FURTHER TAILS

FURTHER TAILS

THE AMAZING STORIES OF GRANDPA LION.

BY N. "Karmakat" Franzetti
Behemel Fatereaver
Xi "Wuffy" Silverwind
Jake Lioner

CONTENTS

FOREWORD

So here is pretty much the second book I am putting out.

Already the first one was surprising to me, but I never thought I would now launch myself into doing a book regrouping short stories with other authors. It does help that said authors are also close friends and it makes it even more pleasant.

This different adventure than my regular novel started after trying to present two different short stories, present in this book, and realizing that at least one of them was way too important for me to not try to get people to read it.

This short story ended up with a part two to tell the truth, and in those two stories mostly, I really poured my heart out. They might be shocking for some people but I hope that it will be mostly an eye opener for people.

Then I decided on a super hero story, and another one about a real friendship whatever it takes.

But I thought it wasn't enough and fair to sell a book that small to people. So I enrolled Behemel and Wuffy, two great authors to my point of view, to give more "weight" to that book if I might call it that way.

I can't say that unlike my other novel, on which I am already working on the second one, that there will be a sequel for this one. But those were stories that we worked on and wanted to share with people.

And to add on that I decided to get another of my little brother into this book. Asking him to use his wonderful mind to do all the art for us. So that's when Jake Lioner joined our crazy group and crazy adventure.

Now we just hope that you will all enjoy it like we did when we worked on it.

N. Karmakat Franzetti
www.furaffinity.net/user/karmakat/
karmakat01.deviantart.com/
www.lulu.com/spotlight/kazenoskara
www.smashwords.com/profile/view/karmakat

Wuffy

Behemel

Jake Lioner
www.furaffinity.net/user/jakelioner83

FURTHER TAILS

THE AMAZING STORIES OF GRANDPA LION.

You take a decision thinking it's to protect others,
but isn't it because you are afraid instead at times...

THE OTHER SIDE OF ME

BY N. "KARMAKAT" FRANZETTI

Most people have a secret. The most interesting part is the very different ways most people treat or live with their secrets. For some people, it's a way to appear "mysterious" and attract others. For others it's just something they don't really pay much attention to, like a part of everyday life. But for some, it's a real burden. They carry a weight so deep and heavy in their hearts that it feels like more weight than a building some days.

Here I am – coughing and bleeding on the floor, a literal building on top of me. Today was supposed to be a good day; I was supposed to spend the day with someone dear to my heart. I even had bought flowers, a gift, and made a reservation at a nice restaurant for fuck's sake. But all that was before my "second life" decided to call me for duty and cause me to end up in this situation.

I try to shift around a little bit, cringing in pain as I do, too slowly pull out the flashlight I carry in my utility belt. Damn. Great I think I have got a few cracked ribs maybe even broken. If that wasn't enough, I have multiple lacerations and pieces of the building crushing my legs right now. I look around myself and I can't decide if should consider myself lucky or not – I am trapped but still alive.

The only reason I am hesitating is that I can't be sure anyone will get me out of here in time or if I will just die slowly in here.

I guess at this point I should introduce myself. My name is Joseph, and I am a thirty two year old lion. I work as a medic in a public clinic, even though I could actually have been a doctor if I had wanted to... or the opportunity. That was before my secret decided to impose itself in my life. I remember that night in July. My eighteenth birthday was getting close, and I was just working on my partials in my second years of surgeon's school. I had pretty good grades, and I wanted to keep it that way so I wouldn't lose my grants. Interesting how life can change with just a sneeze at times?

I had one building up my nose that night while I was reading my book, and when that sneeze came out boy did my world changed. In one sneeze, I had created a wind that blasted the whole wall in front of me out and sent all my furniture flying around. I can tell you that I was really freaked out when I saw what happened, once the dust settled down. I guess I was still a bit lucky it got chalked as a gas leak that day. That was the day I basically discovered I had powers over the wind. And believe, me my freaking out wasn't over by then.

When you grow up in a world with people having super powers, you just look at them and cheer them on, or even dream about having some too. But the day when it really happens out of the blue... that's when you realize your whole life is about to change. After all, my parents weren't crazy scientists and I have never been into a radioactive accident... the only reason I ended up with these powers is because of what they call a "simple" genetic mutation. Simple my ass I swear. Of course at first all I kept hoping was that it was just a coincidence and that would never happen again. But when every time you feel a sense of unease growing inside, or that you are losing your temper and you the wind around you start picking up speed, you just realize you can't keep thinking that.

I was so worried that I would be considered a freak that I decided to drop out of school and to try and learn how to control these powers of mine in the middle of a forest. Through the weeks, I discovered I could not only control wind but also fly thanks to it. And while sort of worst bad at first, I started to develop a kind of super strength. Like one surprise wasn't enough at that point. When I could finally go back in public places without risking the lives of others I had lost my grants for school, so I had to find a job. God did I hate this secret of mine back then.

As I try to free my legs from the pillars and end up coughing up more blood, my mind begins to drift back to the rest of the events that followed. As time went on, more people with super powers started showing up. It would have been interesting if most of them hadn't decided to use their powers to basically settle their grudges against society, or even worst just do whatever they wanted. Over time, most people started to get scared of just going out of their houses. It was getting freaking ridiculous, I swear. That was until some people finally decided to use their powers to protect people. It made me feel like I was living in a kid's comic book.

I remember the day I decided to take part of that fight. I was walking through the park to an interview when a crazy guy started shooting laser beams out of his hands at every one. He kept on screaming how he was fed up with how society kept abusing him, and that god himself had given him the power to avenge people like him. Freaking religious fanatics are everywhere nowadays.

I remember how I ran out in the middle of it all to protect a group of kids that were about to get blasted. Once the kids safely out of the way I turned my attention back to the guy that kept shooting at everything like a lunatic. The wind kept moving faster and faster until I couldn't stop myself anymore. I just grabbed a bench and threw it straight at his head, then decided to cut a tree with the power of wind and made it fall on him, effectively making sure he was pinned down to the ground. Even now I still remember saying, "Take that 'divine punishment', freak" then I left since I didn't want people to know it was me that had done that. I had to keep my identity and secret safe the best I could after all. That was one of the only times my secret hadn't bothered me at all. It was more like I had a purpose now – a real reason to keep it hidden and use it.

A few months later, a new lion in tights was flying through the city. I had made a costume in red and black with quite a bit of work put into it. Who would have thought that Kevlar was such a freaking pain in the ass to find? Then, add some red glasses made with a very special kind of plastic to hide my identity and finally Tempest, the "lion that roars through the wind" was born. I am not even sure why the press decided to add that "moniker" after my name. It's not like I need to roar to call upon the wind for help. It made for a funny situation too, when that "super villain" started to monologue that he would be the one beating me since he had manage to put his hands around my muzzle to keep it shut. That is until I motioned to him to look down, making him realize that I had flown us up about thousand feet in the air, causing him to faint.

I cringe from the pain after giggling when I remember about that time and think, "Okay, laughing is really not a good idea right now." The more I try to get my legs free, the more I realize that it just hurts. If my wind were to create any tempests right about now, all I would end up doing is sending pieces of the building everywhere and possibly even kill or hurt innocent people. Still, I try to move once more, feeling a kind of stabbing sensation on my chest that causes me to pass out and dream about the rest of my life since my new found secret.

When I was younger, I had always made a point to not keep any secrets from my parents at the very least. So before leaving for college, I had decided to tell them what my "big secret" was back then. God, did they take it badly that their only son was gay. They kept shouting words like faggot at me, that being one of the more tame insults. I sure had no problem keeping my other secret from them once I discovered it.

My bigger problem with that new "super" secret, as others like me call it, is how it affects whatever relationships I might enter into. I had a few different ones going on, but they never lasted long. Every time they were said I wasn't taking them seriously enough, and that I wasn't interested in them enough to make it work. Most of them even assumed I was a "player" having sex with everyone I laid my eyes on. That was the biggest problem of this secret. I know why we keep a secret identity. So we can work and have a "normal life" – or as normal as we can get – on the side and protect the people around us as well as we can. But when you want to date someone, that secret really gets in the way...

You can't just say on the first or second date, "Oh, by the way, just so you know, I am also the super hero 'Tempest' so at times I might have to run away and go help people, the city, or even help 'save the world'. Of course you can't tell anyone about it because of the possibility of there being a break up." That would not go very well at all. How many times had I been late due to an attack, or had to leave due to an emergency mid-date because someone was in danger? How many times had I shown up with an odd wound or bruises that I had to find silly excuses for? I was starting to think I would just end up being alone with that secret forever since I could barely keep a social life outside of work.

Until one day, a group of other super heroes decided to contact me and ask me to join them. They were called the "Elementals", and had decided to form an alliance with one another in order to try and gather forces against bigger threats, as well as to support one another and develop new technology. As the name implied, our powers were all related to the elements, we had Solaria, Terra, Aquanaut, Nova, and a few more. We were all dispatched around the world, but were ready to help each other at the first sign of trouble. My secret felt like it was less "heavy" with them. It felt nice having people who shared the same burden. But even though I felt like I could be myself with them, I still felt like something was missing in my life.

Most of them had a special someone by their side; someone they could share very intimate moments with. I couldn't help but be jealous of them on that part. I was openly gay with them because I wanted at least a part of my life to have no lies. And I was damn glad that they understood that I wasn't the stereotypical queer that just going to try and hump them. But still, due to that jealous feeling I couldn't help but stay away from them during social events because it was hurting me to see them so happy together. In those moments to me it felt like I had a deeper burden and secret than any of them.

And that leads me to thinking about him again, that cute and crazy husky I have been seeing for the last two years: Trent. Even though I had super strength, I had decided to join a gym so I could keep interacting with people and also to have an excuse of why my body was so big. Odd how many stuff are implied in the same "packaging" when you end up with this kind of secrets. "You got new powers and super strength? Well you are going to need a full new wardrobe because you will outgrow your old one." First months I seriously considered looking and applying for state subventions just so I could pay for my rent and food. So I was lifting at the gym that day when my attention was caught by him. He was new at the gym, and he sure got a lot of attention from the regular crowed. I was so shocked and attracted to him that I stopped lifting mid lift and started staring at him. A female trainer of the gym even asked me if I ended up stuck or something.

After a nervous chuckle, I decided to try and interact with him by offering to spot for him and show him around. I was doing two hours of training four days a week with him when I finally decided to ask him out. I was lucky on our first dates since my secret wasn't interfering. I was actually able to go out with him without having to run away or be an hour late. But of course that wouldn't last, as work was already on my ass for always being late or running away without much warning but now it was making me feel like I was bleeding inside when I see the pain in his eyes after I tell him I couldn't make our dates. It was burning me inside to not be able to explain him why, and give him the feeling that I was taking him for an idiot each time. At that thought I just wake up and feel ashamed of myself.

Now I might end up dying under a building without ever telling him the truth. He had been by my side for so long, and I might just disappear from his life without an explanation? I know the team would find an excuse of some sort but they would never tell him the truth. I couldn't stop some tears that slowly rolled down my muzzle at that thought. My sweet and caring husky that I am in love with, but couldn't even manage to tell him the truth about me yet, I tried many times to gather the courage for it, but I could never actually take the final step. And now that I am maybe about to die, it hurts even more than the broken ribs.

The pain in his voice when I called him on the phone to tell him I had an emergency without explaining really what it was. This was our two years anniversary today; I wanted to make it special, but instead a scientist freak decided to unleash a giant robot on the city next to ours. I was in such a hurry to try to help that I couldn't even think of any good excuse, and he felt it. I am nearly sure he was crying on the phone when I called to cancel. I am such an idiot I swear.

I could say that I never told him before to protect his life; that knowing about my secret would put his life in even more danger than usual. But that would be lying. The truth is that I am a coward. You would think that being a hero means you have courage, and that you face adversity bravely and without fear. But that is just wishful thinking because even as hero I have a big fear inside my heart. I am worried that the one guy that stayed by my side all those year, and went through all my bad moments, would consider me a freak and run away.

How can it be so easy to say the "L" word, yet so hard to tell the truth about the biggest secret in my life? After all, shouldn't I be proud of what I do? Of the fact that I help people? Thing is that at the end it can still be summed up to "I do stuff that is not natural", and I can't be sure how he will react to it. But at this point, when I see his smile in my memories, I can't help but wonder how will he react when he learns that I died without even knowing why? Will he be wondering why I was in this city? Why I came here, or wound up did I come here so fast... would the other even try to come up with an excuse to hide this damn secret of mine?

At this point, I can't stand it; he is the one who as stayed me by my side. He cheered me up even when he never knew the real reasons why I was down; like a mission that went wrong. All he asked me for was honesty, and I couldn't even give that. I really did want to tell him, but I was scared... so damn scared. How could I have been such an idiot? That guy is perfect, and I kept hurting him by hiding from him one of the most important parts of my life? He kept giving me chances, dealing with my lies and still being by my side. I don't want to die without him knowing why at least. Without him knowing what I fight for, the reason why I do this... I feel like I have to tell him. If I want to make a future with him, I have to share that secret with him. I can't be selfish and I can't keep on hurting him.

That is just not fair for him, what with all he did for me.

I decide I need to get out of here. Even if I die trying or end up broken, I need to find a way out of here. I take a few deep breaths and try to call wind toward me, hoping I can figure out where any sort of exit might be. The wind is moving all around me, letting me know that I am not sealed inside. I try to get my legs free again, but it feels like the weight of the piece trapping me is too much if I don't break it first. Problem is that I can't break it without risking to get crushed more. I take a few deep breaths, breathing slowly so it doesn't as to not hurt as much, while I just whisper, "Please, God... I know I kept lying to him, and I regret it. I really do. If I get out of here, I swear that I will tell him about my secret. I really swear it, God." Then I close my eyes and start seeing images of him, remembering how good he feels in my arms. "Trent... I really want to tell you everything because I love you... and you deserve to know the truth." if wish I could at least tell the others where I am, but of course my communicator got crushed when the building collapsed.

I don't really know why I did that. I just felt like I had to release some of the pain and nerves I had building inside of me. All I know is that without thinking, I start roaring as loud as I can. My chest hurt so badly but I couldn't stop, I just took another deep breath and then start roaring again for several minutes. But of course, I start to cough up blood again because of it.

A few minutes later, a miracle happens. The rubble and leftover part of the building start opening up over me until I see a big lady bear in orange and green tights with a big smile in the light over me. She just chuckles at me and says "Hey there big kitty. I would have thought you would have farted your way out by now."

I give her a big smile and say, "Oh God Terra. Even with your horrible sense of humor, I have never been happier to see you." She helps me out slowly, and while I am using her as a cane I ask, "How is the robot?"

She nods to the direction in front of us, and I see the robot still trying to destroy the city while Nova, Solaria, and Agua – the Mexican version of Aquanaut – are still trying their best to stop it. She then says, "As you can see, it is still up and kicking. The real problem is that Fuse is not able to come right now, and you know he is our best bet against that guy."

I start snarling at that thing that ruined the special day Trent and I were supposed to have together, and I tell her, "I got a score to settle with this one." I let go of her shoulder and start flying right next to her before I add, "Just be ready to catch anything that might fall off. And warn the team please. My communicator broke."

She starts trying to argue with me that I am not in any sort of shape to fight, but I just fly toward the robot while holding my chest with one hand. Once I am in front of him, I look at him and say, "Remember me? Don't worry, round two will be quick." As I finish saying that, I call all the wind I can on his head and start creating the fastest, and most concentrated in one spot, tornado I can. On the other side, I do my best to hold the body in place while the winds on its head turn faster and faster with each passing seconds. As his head starts turning, around I yell at him through the winds, "I AM TEMPEST, AND PEOPLE REALLY DON'T LIKE IT WHEN I LOSE MY CALM!"

Several minutes later, the head starts to successfully unscrew itself from the body and finally breaks when the strain is too much. I do my best to slow down the fall of the head using the winds, but I can't keep the body up too. Fortunately, Terra had listened to me and was ready to take care of it. Once the head got close enough to the ground I wasn't able to hold on anymore and just let it go, falling on the ground along with it. But my teammates were ready for me too, Solaria catching me on the fly before he brings me down next to the others. I look up at Solaria with a small smile; I always liked him and his white and gold costume. I have to say, for a German Shepard he really looks great and is always reliable. Through it probably helps when you are married to someone that knows your secret, and that you work in a family business. He gives me a business look from behind his golden mask and says, "You really did way too much, you know that?" But then he smiles warmly at me and adds, "But great use of your powers. I didn't think you would manage to pull a stunt like that."

I give a small chuckle and hiss from the pain before I tell him, "He made me lose my temper. Today was the worst day for it to show up." The way he gives me a knowing look lets me know that I know I don't have to add any more details to what I am talking about.

In response to that that Terra gets closer to us and says, "Show and tell later 'girls', we need to take him to the base quickly and take care of his wounds."

I try to protest "But... I can't... not right now. I have a promise to keep, I can't keep on delaying it."

That's when Starshine starts speaking through Solaria's communicator "You are the closest thing we have to a doctor we have in the team. But I am no idiot. Your promise might be important, but it will have to wait until we take care of you first." After a minute of silence he realized that I am not trying to argue so he adds, "What do you current your health status is?"

I give a big sigh and say, "On first estimation I would say several bruises, and small cuts, possibly even a sprained ankle, but surprisingly nothing broken in my legs." Then after a second I add, "I think I got three or four cracked ribs and possibly one broken one. The blood spitting is most likely due to a wound in the stomach or esophagus area. However, I don't think that the pain is from a lung perforation due to the ribs."

We hear some typing on a keyboard before he says, "I am getting the medical bay ready to take care of right and opening a portal right now. One of you better be sure he gets there right away, while the others come seem me to file reports."

As promised, the portal opens just in front of us. Solaria and Terra make sure to carry me to the medical bay of our base so I don't risk breaking my damaged ribs even more. They help me out of my costume and set me up on the cold examination table while Solaria make sure I don't try to run away. The buzz of those machines is unbearable to me, and I really can't stand it. I just do my best to not move so it will take as little time as possible. Out of the blue, Solaria's voice takes me out of my daydreaming about Trent. I was just starting to wonder how I could tell Trent the truth about me when he asks, "You found the right one didn't you? The one you want to tell all the truth about yourself?"

I gasp a bit from the surprise and just say, "Yes... I think I did. He is the only one that has stayed by my side for all this time. He helped me through a lot of hard times and never accused me of anything, even if I was obviously lying to him all those times." I look at the ceiling while the machine keeps working on me and I add "I can't keep hurting him with my lies, so even if he decides to leave me I need to tell him the truth. Today was supposed to be our anniversary... two years together, that's a damn record for me. He keeps asking me to move in together and I kept being worried about this 'big ugly secret' of mine. But today... today I wanted to say yes. I really wanted to try." Then I turn my head to look at Solaria behind the controls and add, "...And today I nearly died under that building. I nearly died while still lying to him. I understand if you guys will want me out of the team, but I need to tell him."

At that moment, Starshine arrives in the medical bay and says, "To be perfectly honest, we've been keeping an eye on him lately." I look at the snow leopard in his blue and black outfit with a surprise on my face. He chuckles at me before adding "And even I have to admit, that you couldn't have picked a better guy. He is honest and his background is clean."

To that solaria takes off his mask and gives me a big smile with his big brown eyes and says, "Come on. Let's get you patched up and send you as close as we can to where he is so you can save your anniversary after saving the city."

I start sitting up on the table slowly and ask, "So I can go? I was worried you guys would want to keep me here for a few days."

Starshine come with some materials for a cast and a box of painkillers while saying "You are lucky you only have cracked ribs and that your estimations were correct. You can go as long as you swear to not do any hero work for two weeks. We will take care of your city in the meantime." I nod at him and nearly cry at the good news while they set up a cast around my chest.

Once it's all done, they give me a new communicator and wish me luck before opening a portal that transported me into an alley right next to Trent's apartment. I get in front of his door and wonder what I should do. Should I first check if he talks to me first, or should I just fly in through his window so he knows I am not lying?

I fidget without knowing what to do, holding both the box that holds the gift I had bought for him and the flowers. I am still hesitating a bit when, the door opens in front of me and I look up in surprise and shock. There he is standing in front of me with his ears flat on his head and wearing a tank top with his usual jeans. I can see from the marks around his eyes that he indeed cried, and I feel even more ashamed of myself. I lower my head and say, "Hey."

He just sniffles a bit and says, "Hey to you too. I am glad your important business allowed you to come to actually break my heart in person instead of on the phone. You clean up quite well for someone that doesn't like tuxedos for any occasion."

I look up at him and see his nose twitching a bit. I bet he smells the disinfectant on my fur as well as the other medication, so I simply tell him, "I am here to tell you my secret along with everything about me... if you will let me come in, that is."

He looks at me and while rubbing his eyes he says, "Depends... are you planning to run away on me again? Because sincerely I don't think I can take it anymore."

I start looking down at the ground again and tell him, "The only way I will be running away is if you can't handle my secret. What you are telling me is completely justified, and I am very sorry I waited until now to tell you about everything."

He just gives a small chuckle and asks "Are you going to tell me you are secretly married, and that I was an affair you had on the side?"

I didn't dare look up at him while I say "You might end up wishing this was the reason." He sees I am in pain and decides to give me a hug, but my ribs start hurting me badly again and I give a yelp of pain.

He looks at me with worry in his eyes, and while I am holding my chest he takes me to his sofa. I see his TV is on and he was watching the news about the fight I was in three hours ago. While looking at the TV I tell him, "This might make it a bit easier." I take a few seconds and slowly sit on the sofa with him right next to me. "You saw about the fight against the giant robot I assume?" I ask him.

He gives me a hesitant nod and says, "Yeah. But what does that have to do with your secret? You aren't stalling aren't you?"

I just shake my head slowly while I am playing with the box in my pocket, "I am getting there, I promise." I look him in the eyes and say "You saw that the fight was pretty bad, and one of the 'Elementals' ended up buried under a building due to a whack of the hand of that thing, right?"

He nods again at me and says, "Yeah, everyone was so worried about him until his teammates managed to get him out of there. But then he really got his revenge on the robot and seemed to be more or less okay."

Upon hearing that, I take a few deep breaths and tell him, "Well, he wasn't completely okay. He had several cuts and four cracked ribs." I start undoing the buttons on my shirt before adding "You could say he is on 'sick leave' for the next two to three weeks." And at that let my shirt fall open showing him the cast around my chest.

At first he gasps in surprise at my wounds and the cast before asking "How did... what did you do?" Then I can almost see the wheels turning in his head as he starts putting together what I am trying to say.

I just nod and say very calmly and slowly, "Yes... I am Tempest of the Elementals. That's why I was always so late, or having to run away every time."

There, the secret was out. I still wasn't sure how he would react, but his reaction was pretty interesting. He just got closer to me and pulled my mane into the ponytail I use when I am in costume. To add to the confirmation and show him that I was not lying, I pull out my red glasses and put them on. His muzzle drops while he tries to process all I am telling him. "That's... am I dreaming? I cried so much that I fell asleep and now I am dreaming, aren't I?"

I take off the glasses from my face and shake my head at him. "I wish I could tell you this was a dream. But this is the honest truth. This is the big secret I had to keep hiding from you during those two years." To add to the evidence about all I told him, I use a gentle gust of wind to levitate the flowers I brought for him and make them float in front of him. "I hate to say it, but yeah, this is me. I am Tempest, and your life is obviously at risk with me since I am most probably what most people would call a freak of nature, as one of the top powers of the team." I let the flowers land on his lap gently and lower my head. "I am so sorry, and I can understand if you want me to leave you alone. I've wanted to tell you for a while now, but I kept worrying about it. I love you more than I ever loved anyone, and I would do anything to not lose you. But I can't just switch these powers off, and because of that I can't offer you a normal life with me. I am very sorry."

He comes closer to me and helps me take my shirt off the rest of the way, looking at the cuts on my body and checks to see if the cast is real. "This sure is not the 'classic kind' of secret ..." Then he lifts his hand on my cheeks and massages it gently before adding "But you are not a freak to me at all. You are sweet and very romantic. Your only flaws were the lateness and all the blatant lies you kept telling me, but now I understand why." He leans a little closer to me and adds, "I wish you would have told me sooner for sure, but I can understand that a secret like that can't be said like right away. You need to be sure of the person. And I have to say... I feel damn honored that you decided to accept me in this life."

I move my muzzle closer to his and ask him "You sure this isn't scaring you at all?"

He starts rubbing my mane gently and says, "I am not going to say this is something easy to adjust to. When I was seeing you, or your teammates, in troubles until now I was worried, but I wasn't completely affected by it either. Now I know that the guy that nearly died today is someone that I love and want to spend my life with. So yeah, I will need time to adjust. But it's a small price to pay to be part of the life of the guy I love."

I lean closer to him and give him a soft kiss before I say "I know that you are going to need some time to adjust, but I just want to say I love you. I promise to make it the easiest I can for you."

He leans on me to give me a deep kiss and presses a bit on my ribs in the process, making me cringe in pain. He jumps back and starts saying "Oh, God I am so sorry! I hope I didn't hurt you too badly."

I smile at him with a few tears coming out of the corner of my eyes and say, "From my point of view it was worth it. And nothing compared to the smack of that giant robot. Plus, I know a way to make it easier on me." I pull him into my arms and summon a wind that lifts us both in the air, him resting on top of me "I hope you don't mind dating someone that flies."

He starts giving me that nice laugh of his that I learned to love right away, saying, "This is something else I am going to need to get used to, but it's a nice perk that I think I am probably going to love pretty fast I admit it."

We were floating above his sofa while I kept kissing him and rubbing his head before I tell him, "I have a little something for you." I use the wind to pull out the box from my jacket pocket and give it to him. When he opens it, I look at him and wonder if he will like it.

Inside the box there is a platinum bracelet with a husky and a lion facing each other engraved on the front, while on the back there is an inscription that reads "For the man I love. J. to T.." He smiles at me and gives me a kiss before I start putting it around his wrist. "You sure have good taste" he tells me.

I give him another kiss and say, "I think I have the best taste in men too." He laughs and leans on me while I decide to pop the other question I have in mind. "Concerning that request you kept asking me lately, would you still want to move in with me? Now that you know everything about me, that is?"

He smiles at me and just gives me another kiss before saying "I would love to, believe me. I kept on dreaming of you accepting that request honestly." After that we start to kiss with a happy smile on our faces, the sun setting behind us. Finally, the most important guy in my life knows my secret, and that means the world to me.

*At times you can make interesting encounters when
you aren't expecting it...*

KARMA AND FATE

DUEL OF THE ENLIGHTENED
BY BEHEMEL FATEREAVER

The worlds had always been there. For eons, many worlds co-existed among one another. Some visible, others intangible to the naked eye, much less conceivable to fathom in the minds of men. However, there are those blessed by powers beyond, allowed to walk the lines of these worlds, to discover them. Following the nexus of all worlds, they can freely cross the realms, and discover new possibilities. Through magic beyond, souls of tempered will and strength now meet in a world known for attracting such heroes. A world known only to its inhabitants as ... the Nexus.

The bustling town of Cavanar, a town nestled among the rolling hills that led to the mountains to the north, and sea to the south. It was a town of trade, a nexus for which many traders and marketers come to for information, goods, riches, and other desires and needs. Many creatures wandered this town. Many types of creatures from orcs, bird people, werewolves, bears, and tigers. Most of them shared animal traits. There were some human looking creatures, some elves, and others. This world was a place where all creatures, of all races and origins to meet and live. While not always seeing eye-to-eye, many did in fact live among one another peacefully.

Cavanar was also a tourist spot for not just its trade, but also had wide accommodations. What was most well known for was the coliseum on the top of the hill overlooking the town. Many would gather for tournaments of strength and competition with willing competitors from all over the realms. However, as a result the town would often be plagued by excessive brawls out of the arena as well, sometimes with supernatural results.

One such arrival was a young feline warrior. He was a lion, with fur a mix of ash black and grey. His mane was worn out proudly; a bit messy but radiated a seasoned warrior look. He only wore a pair of light cargo pants, allowing his fuzzy feet and chest to be bare to those around him. It also allowed those to have a good look of his tattoos along his arms and chest, the lion very proud of his physical strength. Despite the appearance, he kept to himself among the town as he sat in a cafe enjoying the sites and people watching. He knew little of how he came here, or where he was, but it didn't matter now. He needed the escape from the troubles of his world. Where better to go than another where others were as ... unique as he was? He sat there at the cafe drinking coffee, people watching.

Emerging into the town was another duo of strangers, and just as interesting. Walking side by side was a burly and muscular black lion. Unlike the other, this one's fur was shaded darker than his, almost midnight black. He wore white clothing that almost looked that of a monk. He wore baggy white pants that cut low to his furry feet and a sash around his waist. He also wore a tabard with tribal markings and a crest upon his chest, leaving his strong muscular arms to show. It was also topped by a large white hood he wore over his head, keeping his identity somewhat of a secret.

The person beside him was a female dragoness. Looking more like a human in stature, but sharing the qualities of a dragon, showing off unafraid. She had green scales upon her elegant body, her wings worn over her back as if they were a cape. Black hair stemmed behind her skull and horns, flowing in the air behind her. Her clothing was a bit noticeable. She wore a black adornment of clothing, styled after a traditional black sorceress robes but more modernized. She wore a black top cut low at the navel, showing off her firm chest, and shape. She wore gloves up to her elbows and fingerless. Her skirt was cut short in the front, allowing her legs to be shown shamelessly save for a small flap short of her thighs. The back was far longer, and trailed behind like a cloak. She walked along her friend closely, her arm clinging to his lovingly.

"I'm glad we tried this door to come here," Syeena said. She tugged Behemel's arm more as she led them into the town. "It seems like a festival here."

Behemel looked over the place, seeing many warriors of species and origins. It was interesting for him, to say the least. "A collection of spirits to do battle with one another. I can only hope it has no ill purpose behind it."

Syeena made a face at him, trying to get him to lighten up. "Oh cheer up. They are all consenting fighters. This isn't like your horror." she said, encouraging him to lighten up a bit. "Besides, we might as well have fun here. See the sights... watch the fights... place some bets."

"And you would be betting on whom, exactly?" Behemel asked, leering at Syeena with the mischief in her eyes.

"You, naturally," she said with a laugh, hoping to encourage him to join in on the fun.

Overhearing some of the talk, Karma had soon come to see them more closely. Save for Behemel's hood, Karma could easily see the distinguished looks of a fellow black cat. His curiosity was peeked as he had never met another black lion before. He took pride in being unique but still, he truly wished to meet the guy. He seemed a bit guarded, but the female dragon seemed very friendly. In fact, he was interested in her too as he rarely saw dragons. Let alone, an anthro dragon. Putting down his coffee, he decided to go and talk to them. He was unsure what he would say, but he didn't want an opprotunity like this to slip him bye. With a calm breath, he proceeded closer to the couple.

"Excuse me," a voice caught their attention. Behemel stopped as he turned to the origin of the voice. He looked and had a hum of amusement in his voice to see who it was. Another black lion much like himself. His tone was polite, but not shy. Genuine curiosity was on his face, a guilty crime that all felines shared.

"Greetings," Behemel said with a nod. "Can we help you?"

Karma raised a hand in denial. "No no… I am sorry but I wanted to introduce myself. Name's Karma. Karmakat Silverwind. I am new here as well. I know this is odd, but I had not found another black lion like myself and wanted to say hello."

He is honest, Behemel thought. He seemed a little bit younger than him, but not by much. Behemel looked him over, taking in his type. He didn't look like him, despite being the same species. Behemel was closer to a more primal type of lion while Karma leaned more to the humanoid type. But both were strong and had an air of power to each of them. Behemel was impressed, and curious himself to find another black lion, even if not from the same worlds.

Syeena, on the other hand, was interested in a far different way. She stepped between them, and she looked Karma over with hungry eyes. "Well hello there, as well. I am curious myself. Never thought I would meet another black cat, and close to Behemel's size might I add," she said, shamelessly sizing him up with her eyes. She was also amused by the lion's lack of shirt and her eyes showing a seductive gleam. It was almost enough to make Karma back up a bit from how assertive she was. Behemel, however, just rolled his eyes and rubbed his forehead. Syeena did enjoy being flirtatious with others. A quality he had long ago accepted as part of her nature. "I'm Syeena Blackrose. Nice to meet you, sugar." she said, leaning closer to Karma.

Karma was a bit perplexed as Syeena approach. He was not used to such forward behavior, especially from women. "Um… hi there. Very nice to meet you, milady." he said in a kind greeting.

Syeena continued to look him over, almost like a predator wanting a meal. She then turned to Behemel, a smirk along her face. " Very nice to meet you indeed," she said but winking at Behemel, who was still trying to deal with her behavior. "You're name's Karma, correct? A worthy name for such a powerful looking cat like yourself."

"Ahem," Behemel coughed, trying to divert her attention. "Syeena, careful. Not everyone is as used to your charms, as I am," he said kindly. "Sorry about her. She is... spirited, to say the least."

Karma did look a bit nervous with the dragon looking him over, but he turned to Behemel a bit with a calmer smile. "It's okay... It's nice to meet you both. Who are you?" he asked.

"Behemel Fatereaver," the black lion greeted. With that, he decided it was okay to lower his hood. Like his arms and feet, Behemel had a darker shade of black fur. He could have easily passed for a panther save for his long mane. Despite a firm complexion, he had a kind look to his eye as he looked to Karma. He then extended a paw to shake the other lion's paw.

The two lion's shook paws, each one's firm of that of a true warrior.

Syeena chuckled a bit under her breath, finding the budding friendship between the two lion's amusing. Cutting in, Syeena once more leaned in towards Karma. The seductive dragoness allowed her tail to tickle the calf of Karma's leg in an enticing manner. Her claws soon took hold of his arm, strong but not bruising as she didn't intend for Karma to back up this time. "I'm Syeena. Syeena Blackrose," she cooed, showing her interest in the lion as well. She soon reached up and ran her fingers through the main around his chest. "Mmmm. You sure are cute. Just short of or about as close to Behemel. Want to hang out a little, handsome?" she said.

Behemel just rolled his eyes. He took no offence of his lover being flirty with others. She always did this with the few she thought caught her eye. He was more amused than annoyed.

However, the surprise on Karmakat's face was evident he had not met such a fast female before. His face showed genuine alarm, embarrassment and confusion. "Um... I uh, " Karma struggled to find the right words before the rather aggressive dragoness. "Thanks— I think. But um... That sounds nice, but I am not used to girls— like this, you know?"

He tried hard to make his point clear, but Syeena could see it. He was genuinely not interested. She gave a shrug of her shoulders and let out a sign of disappointment. "Aw, why do so many cute cats have to be like this," she said with a playful wink at Karma. Both lions' blushed under their black fur. For Karma, it was for being singled out like that. For Behemel, it was for her being so blunt. "Oh well. I understand."

"That's enough Syeena," Behemel stopped her, putting a paw on her shoulder. "You're verging on sexual harassment."

It was her turn to roll her eyes. She was never one to consider that as most people she ended up flirting with was drawn in by her charm and appearance. "Yeah you're right. I would have never imagined that happening by me. Last person to harass me I made him shit his pants before I reduced him to a bloody pulp." She then turned back to Karma and gave a sincere smile and raise of a hand. "Nice to meet you, Karma. I meant no harm."

"Not a problem," Karma replied, shaking her hand while trying to be a gentleman himself. "Anyway, are you joining the free battle?"

Behemel cocked his heat at the mention of it. He blinked, not aware of the event that Karma had now shared with him. "Free battle? You mean a tournament? I knew this town was a warring city for people to show off their strength, but this is the first time I heard of this event."

Karma smiled and crossed his strong arms along his chest. "There is one every few days. From what I learned, people can register to enter mutual fights with other warriors from across the realms." the black lion explained eagerly, looking excited at the idea as he turned to the Coliseum. "People enter to compete and then the next day they are randomly sorted. It's all safe and mostly honorable save for some bad seeds, but most of the time its for trained warriors to test their mettle."

Behemel looked at the arena with mild interest. Syeena, however, smirked with mischievous intent. "You should soooo sign up Behemel," she teased him on, trying to get him to agree. "You are a good fighter."

The dark lion however was more amused to the fact Karma was one of good quality, to be confident enough to join the competition.

He could only assume the gathering of warriors there were of high caliber, magic or sheer might. "You're a warrior too then. It is a pleasure to meet you then. As for joining... I am not sure," he replied, trying to ignore Syeena's teasing.

With a shrug, Karma nodded with mild understanding. "Just saying it is there. Either way, I knew you were a warrior not just by your being here but looking at you. Maybe we can spar sometime?" he asked.

Behemel nodded and smirked from his hood. "I would like that my friend," he said with a humble bow of his head to his new friend. "If you will excuse us, we are going to go explore this town a bit. I'm sure we will meet again soon." the lion said. With Syeena beside him, the two walked on into the town, leaving Karma smiling as he gave a soft wave to them.

While it was not clear then, the two had common threads that bound them through space and time. Fates of close nature.

The soft steam of the hot springs wafted into the night air. The stars twinkled in the alien sky above them; soft streams of colored energy like wisps of clouds passed the sky, showing how different this world's nights were to others.

After having explored the town and coliseum with Syeena, looking over the events of the coliseum and seeing the sites in general, they had reached a pleasant inn that was styled after an oriental theme. The building itself was that similar to Japan's architecture, with paper styled windows and doors that slid sideways. Bamboo like woods provided a natural boarder for the baths behind the inn while rocks and water added to the ambiance of the baths. Soft splashing could be heard as the guests relaxed.

There were two sides. Males and females, both with were otherwise vacant except to the males side where Behemel was. Oddly though, he was not alone as someone was playfully being where she didn't belong. "Syeena, do you enjoy breaking the rules?" Behemel said, mildly embarrassed but also speaking down to her. "If you get caught in here—"

Behemel was soon silenced as Syeena kissed him passionately. She too was in the hot tub, barely adorn with a swim suit around her generous breasts and a thin bikini bottom that revealed her hips and matched her emerald green scales. She shamelessly was pressed up against, clad only by the towel he wore.

"Did you forget I am a thief? I take pleasure in breaking rules," she said, her claws running through his main as the hot water rolled off their bodies.

As she murred against him, the sound of another was coming though. Stepping out from the building and onto the path that led to the hot spring, another person came. It turned out to be none other than Karmakat from before. He was wearing a white towel around his waist also, but the moment he saw through the steam the other lion and the dragoness kissing, his face turned immediately red. He did not expect others in the hot springs. Let alone both the same lion and the dragoness on top of him.

Hearing the presence of the new comer, Syeena stopped and turned to him. "Oh, hi there." Syeena greeted warmly, almost as if what they were doing meant nothing. She just gently pulled away from Behemel while he was still in the water. "Fancy seeing you again. Care to join us?" she said teasingly.

Karmakat averted his eyes, speechless as he didn't know how to respond to the situation.

With a sigh, Behemel sat up, pushing Syeena off him a bit. "Enough. Now you're taking this too far Syeena." he warned, giving her a glare of authority.

The dragoness gave a soft sigh as she pressed her hands against the male's strong chest, muscle beneath the soft fur. "Oh, alright. Can't blame a girl for having a little fun," she said as softly pushed herself off and proceed to stand. She stepped out of the hot springs. "I guess we can have our fun another night. After all, you got a big day tomorrow, right?" Syeena said playfully as she looked at Behemel.

"And why is that?" Behemel asked while cocking an eyebrow at her.

She winked back at him. "Because I signed you up for the coliseum. You're going to need your strength for it. Goodnight." At that moment Syeena jumped out of the hot spring and proceed to swiftly leave. Behemel tried to grab her but nearly lost his towel as he came out and grabbed it. Syeena was out or reach as she strode forward to the exit. Passing Karmakat, she smirked and gave him a light tap on the shoulder. "You too have a good night, hon," she said sweetly before leaving the two alone.

"Wait! I never agreed to—" Behemel shouted to her but she had already turned her back and left.

As she left for the changing rooms, and their room, Behemel let out a strained sigh as he rubbed his head. He soon turned to Karma, rather speechless from the fact she was there in the men's hot baths. "I'm really sorry about her," Behemel said to Karma, "She is well... enjoys challenging the law to be delicate. She can be a handful as you can tell."

"I noticed," Karma said with a strained growl, running a paw through his mane. "I guess I can just come back later—"

Behemel just waved his paw dismissively. "Don't worry about it. Please, don't let that ruin your bath. Come in," Behemel added as he sat back down into the hot water, the water coming up to his chest as he rested his arms against the rocks.

After a moment of hesitation, Karma relaxed and understood. Despite the embarrassment he felt for 'walking in on them' he soon let it slide and proceed towards the water. He gently entered the pool, the heated water washing over his fur and body, a soothing feeling upon his muscles and mind. He sat himself near another pile of rocks, adjacent to where Behemel sat as the two lions both enjoyed the soothing bath. Neither one was uncomfortable with another's presence.

"So you did join, after all?" Karma asked, "The coliseum, I mean?"

A soft growl escaped Behemel, realizing now he was. "Thanks to Syeena's trickery. I had said I wasn't interested in fighting for others' entertainment, but she apparently signed me up when I wasn't looking. Cheeky little devil she is," he replied with a low tone.

Karma laughed at that, a paw splashing into the water. "Very. She seems like a handful," the lion commented, as he began to relax more among his new friend. "She must think highly of you to do that, though. Are you a seasoned warrior?"

Behemel's reaction was quiet but thoughtful. "I had my share of fights, and powers to match against strong enemies. Normally I wouldn't bother with this kind of event, but now it seems I don't have a choice."

The lion of lighter black fur looked to Behemel with confusion as he washed himself with a sponge nearby that was on a tray on the rocks. "But why? I imagine she wouldn't have signed you up if you weren't good." he stated.

"Being good is not the problem. I once fought in an arena, against my own will. And I didn't like it. "

Those words alone were enough to make Karma see his point. It was now clear that Behemel had a dark past as dark as the black fur on his body. His eyes alone spoke of wisdom and experience, laced with a painful past. Karma dropped his enthusiasm, now understanding what the lion meant.

"I'm sorry. I didn't know..." Karma said, realizing the topic struck a nerve.

Behemel let out another sigh and tried to not let the past weigh him down. "It's okay," he said, trying to sound more relaxed and at ease. "Maybe it is time for me to face those fears. Its just... I have had a rough past. Demons I must come to terms with..."

The memories of Behemel were laced with fears. As a cub his village was razed and destroyed, him being one of the few survivors and pulled into the pits of Pandemonium. He was then forced to train as a gladiator for the sick pleasure of the demon observers who attended and to make him into a weapon for their needs. While he did escape, he did so by awakening his own inner rage and laid waste to all that was in his path. The title, the Beast of Pandemonium, would forever haunt him as a reminder of the dark power that dwelled inside him and what he was capable. Something he vowed never to let released again.

Karma looked at Behemel, a look of sympathy and understanding on his face. His left paw rubbed the tattoos that were on his right arm. The markings on his body that kept the demonic spirits that dwelled within him at bay, and prevented him from getting loose. Every now and again Karma would feel its presence, testing the limits of his morals and sanity. But still, through great discipline, training and support, he had kept that influence from breaking him.

"I understand, friend... I know too well what it means to deal with inner darkness. I suspect it's the same for you," Karma said, and soon looked up at the dark sky with the stars beyond.

A long silence hung between them, as they rested. Kindred spirits united in that strange world, both with an inner darkness and powers that strengthened their resolves to overcome it.

Taking water and splashing his face with it, Behemel cleared his mind of the thoughts that weighed him down. Now having to face the arena the next day, he began to wonder just what would happen upon this event. To enter the arena, even for one fight, and to face a worthy foe. The idea to simply test his abilities against another honorable warrior was an idea that Behemel could respect and get behind with.

"I take it, you too, have entered?" Behemel guessed as he looked over to Karma, a smirk on his face.

Karma laughed a bit, flexing an arm to reveal his muscles from the steamy water. "Yes, I have. I practiced martial arts for a good portion of my life, along with some... other tricks," he said slyly, giving Behemel a wink. "And you don't strike me as an average warrior ether."

Modest, Behemel just hummed at the comment and nodded. "We will see, now won't we?" he replied, causing both lions to laugh a bit.

Too warm for comfort from the warm water, Behemel rose up out of the hot spring. He shook his mane, spraying water a bit, and then reached for his towel. Muscles flexed as he stepped out, along his back, legs and arms, and soon he wrapped the towel around his waist. He turned to Karma, a kind smile on his face. "I wish you luck for tomorrow, friend. I think I had my fill of the hot springs," the lion said, a stretch of his maw following with a lion's yawn. "Have a good night," he said and with a nod, turned to head back towards his room where Syeena would be waiting.

Karma watched him leave, rather pleased to have met such a lion like himself. He then placed his paws behind his head and looked up to the sky, the aurora-like sky bringing peace to his soul as he watched. Fate, it seemed, smiled upon Karma to have met Behemel, and would do so for the day to follow.

The sunlight now gleamed overhead as the air was filled with the roar of a enthusiastic and anticipating crowd. The stadium was made in a circular setting, the bleachers filled with many creatures of many races and species. From mammals to insects, these creatures had gathered to witness the events that would be taking place in the center. The arena itself was a dusty hole, with 12 foot tall walls that divided the contestants with the audience, save for the two gated holes in them that allowed people to come and go when not drawn down.

In one of the dark tunnels waited Behemel. *I can't believe I let her talk me into this,* Behemel thought as he rested against the wall. He dwelled of how insistent Syeena was to see him fight, and how she would be waiting to see how he did. Her recklessness and disregard of his wishes was only matched by her faith in him. At the very least, he was grateful for that.

He was mentally preparing himself, allowing his mind to rest before he faced his challenger for the day. The system was that the competitors were paired randomly. Only one fight and the participants were rewarded by the results. Both were paid, but the winner got a bigger sum. Behemel, however, didn't care for the money. He would only fight in a friendly duel to test his strength and measure others. One never knew a person till one fought them.

The announcer soon shouted out the first contestants was to enter the arena. Putting his mind at ease and standing up straight, Behemel soon entered the arena, passing through the gate into the sunshine.

Up in the stands, Syeena was now sitting at the front row to look at the competitors. She rested leisurely, an elbow on the side of the banister as she looked in amusement at the two fighters. Her grin was ecstatic, knowing in the back of her mind this was going to happen.

Behemel had a look of silent surprise as he glared over to his adversary. So did his competitor. On the other side of the arena was none other than Karmakat. The two black lions were now facing one another on opposing sides of the battlefield. Honorable fighters, united and destined to face one each other.

Karma had a look of further surprised and almost burst into a laugh as he saw the cowl of the other black lion. "Well... isn't this an interesting turn of events?" he asked , still laughing.

Behemel gave a sour frown, finding it too ironic to be serious. "Apparently fate, it seems, has a twisted sense of humor," he countered, realizing all the same the friendly lion he had met the day before was now his indicated rival for the fight. The crowd became even more rowdy, eager to see these two muscular jungle cats duke it out. The air was almost electrified as they could feel the power emanating from each warrior.

"Now! Behemel Fatereaver versus Karmakat Silverwind!" the announcer said in the distance, overlooking the fight. "Let the match BEGIN!!"

Behemel exhaled and with it, a white aura radiated off his form. The aura was full of mystical power that Karma had not seen before. It was almost titanic. The lion rose his paw up gently, the aura radiating stronger from it. "Chronos!" Light came from his hand, him channeling the energy around him and towards that point.

As the light lessened, it took the form of an object. In his grasp, Behemel had conjured a silver scythe. The weapon appeared elegant, silver and mithril metals merged in an elegant form that reached up the base to the point where the blade and handle met. From it, the blade curved and along its head and blade's edge, a red glow of energy radiated from that point. It was there, adding sharpness to the blade as the energy blades made it look even more intimidating. Finally, a red jewel was embedded in the blade, almost like an eye.

As he held his scythe, Karma smirked. "Nice little toy you have there, but I hope you don't expect to beat me with just that." he said and soon took up a fighting position, fists ready as he entered a stance that spoke experience and skill. The two stared off, both tense at the power of the other. Even now Karma himself began to radiate a feint aura. Feint but potent below the surface.

Finally, Behemel made the first move. He simply gave a slash of his scythe in the air! From that simple motion, a blast of air like a gale sliced across the arena. Karma held his ground as he saw the incoming attack, the wind becoming sharp and curved like a blade.

The blade collided with the area, and erupted, sending a shockwave through the place and sending a gust outward into the observing crowd. Everyone's felt the gust, causing excited roars and gasps to be heard. As Behemel observed the results, he waited patiently. He didn't use full power. He would never against a friendly adversary, but an inexperienced fighter would easily have some wounds after a hit like that.

However, Karma was no inexperienced fighter.

The dust cleared to reveal Karmakat alive and well. He had a single paw extended, open, raised in his opponent's direction. He had CAUGHT the blade of wind and dispersed it, leaving him unharmed. Behemel had a calm look of surprise, but that was not unexpected.

"A love tap, eh?" Karma replied, amused. He then grinned, lionlike teeth showing. "Allow me to return the favor."

Karma then sprinted forward. He moved fast, crossing the distance of the arena in a matter of seconds. Behemel prepared himself, raising his scythe blade back again for a slash. Then suddenly, Karma became a blur and was gone. Behemel's eyes went wide as he saw this and soon sensed the presence of his attacker. Karma had now slipped behind Behemel, fists raised to deliver an attack. Behemel turned in time to see the lion smirk, and Karma threw his punch.

Behemel just had time to bring the staff part of his scythe up to guard. The force of the punch hit, but to his surprise, the strength behind the attack was far stronger than any normal warrior by strength and appearance. Karma's footing was firm into the earth and the force of the blow was as if Behemel had been knocked back by a massive rock! The black lion skidded back, digging his feet into the sandy ground to slow his skidding. He was half way across the arena, now in its center as he stopped and glared at Karma.

Karma had a grin on his face, pleased with himself. He was far stronger than his appearance allowed.

The two lions glared at one another from across the space, both acknowledging one another's strengths. Meanwhile, Syeena was up in the stands above, leaning over to see them. "Come on! You two, make this good! I got money riding on one of you!" she teased, partly to cheer for them and partly to mess with them.

In a moment like this, Behemel blocked out all distraction. His meditative mind worked to focus on his foe, and so did Karmakat, him doing the exact same thing. Both got a good gauge of one another's strengths.

This time, confident, Karma took off to attack again, this time, Behemel blinked as he saw alight a glow. It couldn't be... but it was. Fire. The lion's arms were now aglow with fire as he threw a punch to strike Behemel. With two fingers, Behemel focused his own magic, the power of his weapon that manipulated the wind. Air lashed around him, forming a barrier that dispersed the fire, but it didn't stop Karma's advance. The lion also now crouched low and delivered a sweeping kick. The barrier of wind didn't stop that, and followed by flames trailing behind the kick.

Behemel jumped high, evading the kick as best as he could. The heat of the flames licked at his feet as he flipped upward. With a mental command, he made the scythe in his hands vanish. The light of it divided and soon took the shape of twin blades. As Behemel landed a few meters away, the blades crackled with electricity, sparking every so often.

"What kind of tricks are those? Multiple weapons is bordering on an unfair advantage," Karma said with a touch of playful intent. He rose to his full height.

Behemel narrowed a look at Karmakat. "I'm a Spiritualist. I have the ability to channel the will of different gods and deities into weapons called Spirit Arms, embodying their powers." he explained as simply as he could. He readied his blades, the electrical discharge of them sparking even more to reveal flickering bolts of electricity along the edges. "For example, the scythe I possessed earlier is a manifestation of the ancient god, Chronos. These blades are the embodiment of the angel of lightning. Ramiel. "

He then sprinted forward, his blades at either side of him. The lightning soon spread from the blades to his limbs and up, soon surrounding him in electric energy. In a flash like lightning, he vanished from one spot to the next. Whether the electricity sped him up, or if he was literally jumping with the bolts of lightning, it was impossible to tell as he moved so fast!

Karma had his eyes darting, following Behemel as his lightning like form jumped across the battlefield, almost dizzying. Finally, the flash of lightning end, to show the lion was gone. He sensed a danger above him. He quickly looked up to find Behemel in the air above! The black lion held both swords out, and then flicked his arms. He threw the two twin blades at Karmakat's direction. Oddly, the two blades struck the ground, one on either side of Karma.

Crap, Karma thought as he acted quickly. He dashed forward, just as the sparks from the swords discharged. The two acted like lightning rods and just as Karma had got out of the way, the two activated. Bolts of lightning danced in the air between the two blades, forming a field of electricity that would have electrified the lion if he remained.

After the fierce display of lightning, Behemel landed, and the blades that he had thrown into the ground soon vanished. He looked as Karma regained his stance, turning to his foe. Behemel let out a soft chuckle as he looked at his foe.

"Nice hair," he commented lightly, trying hard to not laugh.

Karmakat blinked and looked up. His main and some of his fur was suddenly standing on end. The electric energy from just a moment, while it didn't hit him, certainly electrified his fur enough to make it stand on end. He let out a small growl and used a paw to flatten out his mane. "Very funny, pal," he growled, gripping his fists tight.

His scowl of irritation turned into a grin. "I think I will show you just who you are messing with," he said and from his gloves he wore along his paws, they began to glow. From them extended a bow staff made of light, much like how Behemel conjured weapons from his force of will. He then charged again, aiming to attack Behemel with his staff.

Behemel used his magic and redrew Chronos, the glistening scythe once again in his hands. This time, however, Karmakat was prepared. The lion lunged forward for close quarters, using his new staff to parry and block Behemel. He used the pole to prevent him from swinging and kept close. Before Behemel knew it, the two were locked together, Karma trying to swing his legs between Behemel's and attempting to trip him up. While he moved and countered, the two were locked together. They both fought around their knees while they struggled to keep one another's weapons from hitting him.

Finally, Karma locked his left leg around Behemel's right, and then shoved. The two lions fell, and soon Behemel was on his back, Karma on top of them as they both pressed their pole arm weapons against one another, their faces inches apart.

"Ah so you're not that good at hand to hand combat, eh? Don't be too embarrassed that I am the top cat here," Karma said playfully, a wink in his eye as he looked down at Behemel.

The black lion pushed over and soon with a grunt, pulled a leg back! Karma soon felt the move and felt as Behemel delivered a fierce kick, enough to send him flying off. The two were separated, Behemel still on the ground. He then spun around, a foot trailing in the dirt and kicking up a dust cloud as he readied his weapon once more.

Now facing one another, both warriors were short on breath. They surprised by one another's powers and resourcefulness. Admiration was shown between them both. "You're not too bad. Better than I could of thought." Behemel was the first to admit.

Karmakat panted, still holding his staff made of spiritual power. "Heh... you're good, yourself." he commented.

The crowd began to cheer louder, enjoying the fight between the two warriors. The tension was building, as the two warriors, from different worlds, from different times, now faced one another as friends, and rivals. The two were now growing stronger, the powers of the two black lions building as they both desired to see more of one another's power.

"Ready to see who is the better warrior?" Karmakat said with a toothed grin.

Behemel smirked. "Sure, let's see who is a step above the other," he commented.

As their auras grew stronger, brighter, they soon sprinted for one another. The crowd was in suspense as they fought, leading to a blinding flash of power and strength, blinding as they clashed!

Karma and Fate intertwined. Allies and rivals discovered. The future for these two... perilous and uncertain as they face the darkness and themselves as well...

When you start your life being rejected it's hard to believe someone can accept you...

INSIDE OF ME

BY N. "KARMAKAT" FRANZETTI

Part 1

Another day in this life... just another day walking through the streets and trying to understand why... or what I could do about it. I take my time walking through the streets as I head toward my destination, and reflect about those last few months.

Feeling the cold as I go through the streets, I decide to stop at that coffee shop that changed my life in so many ways a few months ago. I get a cup of coffee and decide to sit at that exact same place I was back then when it all happened.

My name is Jason, and I am what people would call a regular lion; I like to work out and let my mane grow long, nearly to my hips. I always loved the feeling of being able to play with it while I am thinking about different subjects. My ponytail is, what most people refers to me as classic "art wanker" in a way, even if my clothes don't really fit the description. Since I prefer to wear regular jeans and dark kinds of shirts, most people don't really guess my "specialty" when we first meet, since I generally don't stand out of the crowd. At thirty two years old, I have been able to breeze through most of

my studies without really worrying about them. In so many different ways people consider me pretty successful; I got a good job as an
art professor, with some very good kids in a public school. It leaves
me, enough free time, on the side, to work on my personal pet pro-
jects, and do some art presentation with various degrees of success.
I try to avoid interviews every time I can manage to because they
always ask the same question: "And concerning your personal life?
Would you consider yourself as successful?" It's always the same
question that makes me freeze and feel cold inside... all of that because of the secret I have. I will never forget that summer when I
was a kid. My mom and I were at the beach and I must have been
around twelve years old to the oldest when she had asked me to
come sit next to her to have a talk.

At first, when she told me about it, I didn't understand the im-
plications. I was just a dumb kid with a smile on my muzzle and
dreams- crazy or not- about future. So, as usual, I took it with a
smile and just said something along the lines of: "Ah... okay, can I go
play now?" before my day just went on like nothing happened. It's
only when I got closer to puberty that the weight of that secret hit
me like an anvil. Except unlike in cartoons, every time that figura-
tive anvil hits me I can't just get up and walk away as easily. The first
time I realized the depth of this secret of mine I couldn't stop crying. I think I barely ate anything or got out of my bed for about a
week that time. The few people that I considered friends at the
dorm back then that got really worried for me just kept chalking it
up to bad luck, and say things like, "Next time it will work much
better and you will find someone that's fits a lot more with you." But
well none of them knew about my secret either.

I sip on my coffee to try to warm me up inside, trying to gather
up the courage to get up and do what needs to be done. But at that
moment I see a couple walk inside the coffee shop, and I can't take
my eyes off them. One of them is a stallion; his booming laugh
nearly shakes the windows around him while he just flexes his muscles for the shorter tabby cat that is right next to him. They are
clearly together and look very happy like that; the tabby cat passes a

paw under the stallion shirt while they pick what they want from the menu. The reaction of the stallion is just too give another one of his big laugh and lift the cat in his arms to give him a kiss in front of everyone. For them, it's just normal. Life is just as good as it can get for them right now. Then again neither of them has a secret creeping around their mind that is ready to ruin that joy.

Looking at them, I start thinking back to my first "boyfriend". After a series of rejections, I had decided to simply keep my secret as it was supposed to be... hidden. I decided that maybe if I waited a few dates before I tell them about it, things might work out better. Maybe if they knew me first and got to appreciate me then the secret wouldn't weight as heavily on us, and I would have a chance. I had gone out with that guy, a wolf, for something like a month and a half. He was into art too, but had specialized in acting and especially drama theatre. I remember the first time I met him. It was because his group needed help with creating the scenery for their next play, and they had liked my work. At first, I was paying about as much attention to him as I was the others. I was coming to the get-togethers and setting up the plans for what they had in mind, as I was already used to be working alone by then. But after a few get-togethers I started to acknowledge him. He was always dressed up in such a way that it was pretty much impossible to not notice him. He was always wearing tight clothes, showing off his muscles and fur... and he seemed to make it a point to "run into me" regularly. He even started to come help me do the painting for his group, we spent so many late nights working together while laughing and talking. Nights were pretty much our "secret gathering" after a week, even if we kept working until four am. We never backed out of it until the night when he kissed me by surprise.

At first I wanted to push him away, but I couldn't make myself do it. I just started kissing back, and just considered myself a "normal person" for once. 'Maybe this time my secret won't be as much of a problem' I thought. Though as we went through our dates, I was feeling more and more self-conscious about the fact that I should tell him. But I wanted to be greedy, or even maybe selfish, for just this time. I thought it was love back then, I thought maybe he was the one that would accept me for who I am.... Until that dreadful night. When he asked me to come over to his apartment before we went out for dinner together... I swear I was such an idiot.

For me, it was just another one of our regular dates, where I would meet him at his place. Then we would probably make out a bit and talk about our day before we go out to share a nice dinner together and keep on talking. But I should have known something was different when I arrived to his room and there were candles lighting up the place in different strategic spots. I started to have doubts in my mind, but I kept telling myself "It's probably just a romantic dinner". I couldn't keep on thinking that when he showed up in front of me shirtless and with his zipper open. Before I could say anything he jumped on me and started to take off my shirt, while telling me stuff like "I want to make this night special for us." With his whispering in my ear and both his hot breath and scent on my fur I had a very hard time thinking straight. He was about to attack my pants, and I kept telling him to stop. To him it was just the cute and shy side of me, and he tried to convince me by starting to nibble on my neck a bit more harshly, as if trying to take control. When I felt the pain on my neck my brain kicked in again, and I pushed him backward more roughly. I was glad that I'm bigger than most people; otherwise I don't think I would have been able to get him to stop, let alone grab his attention. He was against the wall looking at me with big eyes, not understanding when I told him, "First we need to talk... there is something you need to know."

I remember the cold shiver that was going through my spine while I was looking at him. I kept taking deep breaths and I started to look down at my shoes. At that moment, he really made me believe that he could have been the one. Seeing that I was about to panic, he came over to put a comforting hand on my shoulder and told me in a soothing voice, "What is it? You know you can talk to me about anything." So I looked at him in the eyes, with a small smile, and I told him my secret. Told him about any details I ever knew or learned about it, anything to try to make it easier on him, and hopefully on me. The first few minutes after I was done I thought it was a good sign that he didn't interrupt me. He was listening, that was supposed to be good right? I gently reached over to grab his hand with mine, tried to give a gesture to make him understand it was still me. But this is when all hell broke loose on me.

His first reaction was to take away his hand from me, and then give me a punch without more warnings. I took a few steps backward due to the surprise, and was holding my jaw with my hand while looking at him. God... the hate in those eyes. His eyes alone were hurting me a thousand times more than his punch. He was snarling at me, and nearly trying to make a hole through my head with those eyes. Then he took a step forward and kept on punching me for several minutes. All that time he just kept saying things like, "How dare you do this to me.... how dare you get close to people!" all those weren't even real questions but plain accusation. I couldn't stop crying as those words were hitting straight into my fears like a knife. I was bigger than him; I could fight back, or even just protect myself. But I couldn't get myself to it. To me, all he was saying was partly right, even if I never asked for that secret. A few minutes after he started punching me, he seems to realize that he was touching me again and just yelled to me "GET THE HELL OUT OF HERE!" So I grabbed my shirt and jacket and ran away in the night, while crying my heart out. The next month after that I was like a zombie drifting through life, always avoiding contact with people around me when I still had a choice at least. I had decided to make myself a promise... never again.

As I continue looking at the stallion and the tabby cat and thinking about those past events, I don't even realize at first that I am crying again. It happened nearly ten years ago, and it still hurts me; his face and reaction are still engraved inside my mind and heart deeply. I look down to try and stop the tears that are flowing down my cheeks for several minutes, hoping my mane is enough to hide my face from the world. I think it didn't really do a great job as one of the waitresses comes next to me and gently asks "Would you like another coffee, sir?" while handing me a napkin. I use the napkin to dry my tears and give her a small nod, not wanting my voice to crack up should I reply to her vocally. A few seconds later, she comes back with my coffee and a chocolate muffin, and with a big smile says, "I added some chocolate syrup in the coffee, sir. The muffin is on the house."

I am a bit surprised by that, but I give her a gentle smile and say, "Thanks a lot." Just a few little words managed to calm my tears and bring me back into the present. And that brings me back to the situation I am in now with Casey. I had spent the last eight years alone, doing even a pretty good job at it. I was friendly and staying professional at work, but making a point to don't let anyone get to close from me. Women were definitely easy. Guys weren't always, but I was getting pretty damn good with my "sentimental wall". I had even made sure to apply at a school with teens so I wouldn't have any temptation of any sort. All of that continued until four months ago when I met him here, in this coffee shop.

I was working on grading the latest assignment I had given to my students while drinking coffee to stay awake. It's impressive how much crap at times a student can write just to add some "filling" to an assignment. I kept on sighing and making faces to myself while playing with my mane – to the point of turning it into a knot – until I heard someone chuckling from the next table. I looked up, mostly by reflex and curiosity, and saw him at that other table. He was openly staring at me with a big smile on his muzzle and with a hot chocolate in his hands. At the moment I saw him it was like the earth stopped, the rest of the world was gone. I couldn't keep my eyes off him. He was a big gray and reddish husky, with a big smile nearly joining both his cheek ruffs. His muzzle and the tip of his ears were a darker grey, and I could see that same color disappear down his sweatshirt. His tail was wagging excitedly behind him as he turned himself on his chair to face me. At that moment I realized I was openly staring, and I felt the heat go up my ears so I just gave him a smile and tried to look down at my papers again. The words on the paper were a blur to me by then, and I couldn't manage to concentrate on it anymore. I closed my eyes to take a deep breath when I heard something that made me jump. "Let me guess. You are a teacher and you are trying to grade your students' papers right?"

My head shot up right away as my muzzle dropped open; he was now in front of me with that big smile of his on his face. And even with his clothes on, I could easily see that see that he worked out a lot too. I started staring at him again, and suddenly a coughed to regain my composure while I grabbed for my coffee. He was still waiting for an answer, so I gave him a smile and said, "Yep, you got me. Impressive how some students can manage to get me to the point of ripping my mane out with their work."

He looks at me and gives me a cute smile from the corner of his muzzle before saying "Well it would be a shame to ruin such a nice mane." Then with another chuckle he gestured to the chair in front of me and added, "Do you mind if I use this seat?"

I look around the coffee house and realize the place is not exactly what you would consider full right now, but I still decide to be friendly with him. He looks like a very nice guy, so I gather my papers to make room for him and tell him, "Sure go ahead. This is, as they say, a free country after all."

He gives a soft laugh as he sits in front of me and says, "I sure hope so... I work very hard for it." Seeing the look of surprise on my face, he laughs a bit harder and adds, "I should probably mention that I say that because I am a cop."

I give a small chuckle and tell him, "That sure explain a lot." I then grab my cup of coffee and start sipping it slowly, continuing to stare into the deep blue color of his eyes. I remember his reaction to me watching him very well. He cocked his head sideways in such a cute way that I started blushing and said, "Should I consider myself in trouble of any kind then, officer?" The moment I said that, I can't suppress a shiver at the possibility that maybe some parents at school discovered my secret and decided to sue me for putting their kids at risk.

At that question, he just gives me a warm smile and says, "As far as I know, I am more of the bad boy here since I laughed at your faces without introducing myself." He then offers me a hand and says, "My name is Casey."

I look at the hand in front of me and hesitate for a minute. In a way, this feels very inviting to me. I feel compelled to feel his fur and warmth at least on my hands, but my secret kept creeping in the back of my mind. But he seems so friendly that I think I can at least do the same, so I grab his hand in a firm way and say, "Pleased to meet you. My name is Jason." While we shaking hands, we look at each other's and I feel like I want to just jump in the "pool of his eyes" before we finally let go after a longer time than was probably needed.

I remember the time we spent talking together that day, while I was being very careful to not let him confuse our drinks. Later on I remember that I shouldn't be letting him get too close to me again, so I make an excuse of having to pick up papers at school and leave it at that. That guy seems really nice, but I feel like because of my secret I can't let anyone near me that way once again. Little did I know that I would find him again at that same coffee house two days later waiting at that very same table. The moment he sees me his smile lights up the room, and he invites me over for another cup of coffee. I didn't see how I could say no without being a jerk, so I agreed and sat with him all afternoon. By the end of the afternoon he was sitting right next to me and seemed to be blushing a bit when he asked, "Would you like to come see a movie with me?"

I gave him a surprised look. In a corner of my mind I kept dreaming about something like this. It had been so long since I had left myself had so much as a friend get so close to me. But with him, the barrier I put up seemed to crumble away. I agreed to his offer with a big blush and we go to the movie place right across from the coffee house. During the movie, something I have been missing more than I ever imagined – and at the same time dreading – happens. Half way through the movie he grabs my hand gently and puts his head on my shoulder. It feels so nice, but at the same time I feel like I should be jumping away from him. Knowing the secret in the back of my mind, I feel like I should hear alerts in my head. Feeling his warmth against me and smelling his scent, I find myself enjoying it but still I know I should get away from him, so I slowly turn my head to give him an excuse like I got a cramp or I have to go use the restroom. Anything to get out of this situation when something happens that I really wasn't expecting; the moment I turned my head to whisper in his ear he lifted his and started kissing me. At that moment my brain just surrendered, it had been so long I haven't felt anything like this that I couldn't even consider stopping it. I just put my arms around his neck and pulled him closer to me, while we are holding the kiss. The kiss was unbelievable. I didn't even feel like stopping to breathe at that moment. I just want it to go on, suck every second that I had been missing it until my brain starts to wake up.

I realize a few minutes later what I am doing; all the stuff I am going to put myself through, and worst of all to him. I just pull away and I am panting to regain control of myself while he looks at me not understanding what happened. The alarms were literally screaming in my head, my secret was reminding itself to me in full force now, and I couldn't escape it. So I wound up doing the only thing I could think to do at that moment – I run away from the theater, leaving him alone without another word or an explanation.

I stir my new cup of coffee as I enjoy the aroma and take a bite of the muffin while I keep remembering the events between us. It's been three days since I ran away from him that evening, and I have done my best to not go back to the coffee place even in case. I was in class working on getting everything ready for the next test when someone knocked at the door. I gave the permission for them to enter, and as I turn around I froze on the spot. In front of me, in his full policeman outfit, was Casey standing, his eyes hiding behind a pair of dark sunglasses. As he stands there in front of me I am not sure of what to say but he decides to speak first. "Hey, I promise I am not here to arrest you still, nor am I stalking you." He takes a deep breath and then ads "I just wanted to say I am sorry I went to fast the other day. It's just..."

My God, I am the one running away like a jerk, and he comes here to apologize. I don't let him finish his sentence; I just cut him off and tell him, "It's not your fault!" It came out much louder that I was planning, but it did manage to stop him in his track. His reaction was to cock his head sideway in that cute way that I love then starts taking off his sunglasses. And I already see that he doesn't understand what I mean with just how his deep blue eyes look at me. So I simply add, "It really wasn't your fault... I am the one with issues. I am sorry I ran away on you like that... I should have tried to..."

This time it's his turn to stop me in my tracks as he comes over to me, taking me in his arms and kissing me once again. It's been so long since I started repressing my feelings that once again my brain goes into overload. Without even thinking about it, I just grab him in my arms and lift him up, making him sit on one of the desks next to me while I am almost literally feeding on our kiss. When we stop and we are both panting he smiles at me and runs his hand through my mane before saying "You might have issues, but I would like to see you again... and I think we both need to get back to work."

I think about what he said while chuckling at it and put my hand on his knee, and start thinking, just for this time, just once I want those alarms in my head to stop. It's not like there is anything wrong in seeing him a few more times after all, right? I look deeply into his blue eyes and nod at him before I end up saying "Tomorrow afternoon I finish at five. Should we meet each other at the coffee place again?"

In return he gives me a big smile and says, "It's a deal Jason... and I really want to help you work on... those issues." Then he bends over and gives me another soft kiss. At the moment he is gone I can't help but think, "My God, what have I done?" I considered canceling or even not showing, but even with my big secret I feel like I would be a coward if I do that. So at that point I had worked up a new plan: go on a few dates and then tell him that, for whatever reason I come up with at that time, that it can't work between us.

How could I have imagined that, during all those months, I would get more and more attached to him? I had always done everything to keep people at bay, but with him one date became two, then three and so on. It's been a month by now, and we call each other the big

"BF" word. I love all I learned about him. I love spending all my free time with him. He even agreed to model for me, and people keep saying they are some of my greatest works for God's sake. He really took a big place in my heart and life, and I feel that now I have a better idea of what love really is. But there is still one big problem... the biggest of them all. He still doesn't know my secret.

Until now I always managed to stall the questions about us being more "personal". We spend a lot of times in public places, but I always managed one way or another, to not have to go to his place or have him suggest going back to mine. But he keeps asking me, trying to make weekend plans for us to do all the stuff we should be doing by now. Two days ago we even had a big fight about it. He kept asking me to spend the night with him, and I kept finding the worst excuses in the world to not do so. He got so pissed at me that he even asked me if I was seeing other people.

He retracted that accusation when he saw that horrified look in my eyes at that assumption, saying that he was sorry. But I was feeling more and more like a jerk – someone that didn't deserve him. So, once again, I did the only thing I could think of: I started crying and ran away again like the big coward I am.

As I munch on my muffin slowly, I look at the people around me and I feel like I am on the verge of crying once again. And I start asking myself that same question I been asking myself for years; "Why do I have to keep this big secret?" As usual, I don't get any enlightenment as an answer to my question; no miracle reason comes through from above to tell me. I am all alone with muffin crumbs, the rest of my coffee, and a hole in my heart because of it. A hole that only one person managed to fill after all those years, but I most probably ruined everything.

The more I think about it, the more I realize I can't leave things hanging like this. That guy has been the nicest to me in a long time. And right now, since I have been avoiding him and his phone calls for the past two days, I can't imagine in what state he must be. Maybe he already hates me, and I would just make it worse by explaining to him why. Who am I kidding at this point? I will definitely make it worse if I tell him my secret now. But I can't keep hiding it. I have to tell him and face whatever reaction he will have. Even if he beats me up I won't even try to resist. He just deserves to know the truth, even if that means he leaves me and becomes little more than a memory for me.

As I think about it I realize more and more that it's the right decision, even if it means a definite end for us. At least I will have good memories to warm up my heart for a while more, or a definite closure toward another relationship. I slowly get up and start to put on my jacket before I go pay the nice waitress from earlier, by living a nice tip for her and giving my best imitation of a smile. When I open the door, the warmth of the sun really picked up but I still shiver due to the cold feeling in my heart. The secret is slowly eating my soul with every step I take toward Casey's house. The closer I get to my destination the more I start to feel the hatred towards my secret; the biggest reason my life has been ruined over and over again. The reason why I don't get near other people and why I might be losing the first guy in years that really made me feel "human" in a way. Once the hatred quieted down I start tasting despair in my muzzle. I consider ripping my heart out once I told him the truth to be done with it so I just never have to go through it again. Would anyone really miss me if I did... at this point, I doubt it.

Then for my usual "dessert" I get the company of misery in my mind. I feel the pain of all the good moments we both had and could have had for the years to come if it wasn't for this... secret. But here I am, at the main entrance to his apartment. I scan the name and numbers and see his name. I slowly lift my hand and hope for a second that he won't be home before I ring. Of course, my luck is absent as usual. A few second after I rang he answers on the speaker asking "Who is it?"

I swallow loud enough, to the point I hoped the microphone wouldn't pick it up at least, and then I slowly say "It's me... Jason. I need to talk to you ...but only if you agree, of course." Without any other answer, he opens the door and I make my way to the fourth floor. The elevator makes me feel like I am on my way to my death at that point with the speed it's going at.

When the doors open and I start to step out, I soon find myself wrapped in the arms of the man I was just about to see, him apparently waiting for me. I hold him tight, in case it's the last time I can, and then he suddenly starts saying, "I am so sorry... I am so very sorry... I shouldn't have doubted you. Please forgive me."

At that moment I am shocked. Once again, I made him feel like it was his fault when I was actually the jerk in all this. I lift his muzzle gently and tell him, "Well... like last time it's not your fault at all. Can we go inside your apartment... I need to tell you something about me."

He looks at me with worry in his eyes but still manages to nods and guides me to his place. I sit on the sofa while he comes and sit next to me. I am holding my hands tightly together while looking deeply at them, not daring to really look at him. We stay in silence for several minutes until he says, "Are you breaking up with me?"

I don't even dare to look up and see his big blue eyes again; I just keep staring at my hands. Eventually I simply say "After I tell you my big secret... you will probably be the one breaking up with me." I take a deep breath and then I add, "Please, this really isn't something easy for me to say. To tell the truth, it always ends up badly for me when I talk about it. So please, let me say what I have to without any interruptions, okay?

I stole a quick glance at him which was just enough to see him nod before looking back down at the floor again. I take a deep breath and then I start explaining myself to him. "Like I have just said, I have a big secret. A few years after I was born, a doctor decided to save money on medication and I ended up infected with a deadly virus." I felt the tears starting to come up out of the corners of my eyes, but I force myself to go through with my explanation. "Since then, I have been to the clinic several times. As you can see I am more or less healthy. The biggest problem, however, is what is inside my body. I have this virus creeping inside me, and not only I do not know how much time I have in my life... but also it can be dangerous for others. I have been following a strict medication for a few years now. I have gone through a lot of side effects because of it especially during the first months. And I don't wish that on anyone especially, not you."

Now that I emptied the weight of my secret from my heart, the tears start flowing out. I couldn't manage to control them but between a few sobs, I still continue telling him, "I should have told you sooner. I am sorry I put your life in danger. I just felt like I really started to love you, even after closing my heart to others." I rub my eyes with my sleeve and add, "I will completely understand if you hate me right now – if you want to punch me even. But I wanted you to know none of all this was your fault; I was just being greedy and a coward... I just let myself fall in love with you, even when I knew perfectly well that I shouldn't."

I didn't dare look up at him. I am so worried to see the same horror in his big blue eyes that I have seen before. Those blue eyes in which I saw so much softness and kindness... I am scared to see hate in them now. After a few seconds with only hearing our breathing I finally hear him shift around on the couch. I brace myself and wait to be punched, but something unexpected happens. He just holds me in his arms and cries on my shoulder. After a few seconds he says, "I am so sorry you went through all that alone... I should have known."

I look at him with surprise, and then tears start flowing down my cheeks while holding him tightly against me. "Does this mean it actually doesn't bother you?"

He looks at me and says, "It bothers me in the sense that the guy I fell in love with is sick. It doesn't bother me at all for myself."

Hearing that makes me start crying even more. All the tears from my heart are draining from all the years I was holding them back. I start to softly kiss him before I push him back on the couch. I stand on top of him and kiss him like it's something that I need for my survival. He is even more important than the air I breathe at that moment, and the way he kisses me back makes me feel that it's the same for him.

We stay kissing like that without moving for several minutes. We are just cuddling while I listen to his heartbeat and breathing, staying on top of him while he holds me tight. I just feel his fur and fill my nostrils with his scent; to me the world feels finally complete for the first time in years. It's like a fairy tale, something you see generally only in movies. I am even at the point I want to pinch myself, I am wondering if all this could only be just a dream, or maybe I died on my way to his place and this is now my own personal heaven.

While I am thinking all that, I just decide to give him another soft and tender kiss. Once we break that long kiss he just asks me, "Would you agree to stay for the night this time?"

I look at him with a big giant smile and nod before I say, "For as long as you want me around. I love you."

He smiles back at me with a tear coming down his cheek before he says "I love you too." and then kisses me tenderly again.

Now I know I can face interviews and tell them, "Yes, I consider myself successful in my life and my work. I met my other half, and I am fully and completely happy now."

You have to remember the ones you love and take the right decisions for their sakes... or yours.

INSIDE OF ME

BY N. "KARMAKAT" FRANZETTI

Part 2

It has been another one of those nights. It's now four in the morning and I've been staring at the ceiling since at least an hour.

After a year of being boyfriends we decided to live together. With the sales of my artwork I had managed to get us a loft in a nice corner of the city and we moved in. Life became amazing, and I was finally happy. I had told Casey everything about myself; I shared my secret with him. I told him what was lurking inside me and still accepted me. I became the happiest person with him by my side. Casey comforts me and I love having him in my arms. He has given me all that I have ever wanted, all that I ever missed in my life. Company, comfort, love, laughs.

Three months later it started going downhill.

I lost my appetite. I found myself sleeping more and more. I tried to be as active as I could by going to my art shows and by losing myself more in my work. But after awhile I found myself falling asleep or talking utter nonsense. It was as if my brain wasn't functioning anymore.

Then one morning it was the worst.

I remember seeing a glimpse of Casey, running around like a lunatic then a nurse coming to see me and taking some of my blood. Then my doctor came it to check on me and that's the last I can remember. It all went black. I was in the darkness and feeling nothing...

When I opened my eyes again I was back at the hospital, in a sterile white room in the middle of the day. I was reliving the memories of pain and all the tests. When the nurse saw that I was conscious she ran to page the doctor. In an instant he was by my bedside, explaining to me that the virus inside my body had moved into attacking my brain cells. He also said that the course of medication I was now on was helping me to get better.

The hospital had called Casey and an hour later he was by my side crying and so grateful that I was back with him. Imagine my surprise when I discovered that Casey had managed to stay by my side for a whole month. He said he was here with me as much as he could but he couldn't always get someone to cover his shift at work. As understanding as they were of the situation, they still had families, too. I understood but I was feeling bad that I had hurt him again. The doctor was doing his best to give us hope by saying that my condition was under control but I still had to undergo many more tests. It was one longer month in that lonely room, being alone with my thoughts all day long. The only joy was that I got to see Casey a few hours every evening. During that time drawing came with difficulty; I was too depressed and worried. Not for me, but for Casey. I was just grateful at this point that I didn't give him my same problems.

When I got out of the hospital I thought I could manage to make amends with him. Casey and I were spending a lot more time in each other's arms. But the medications that the hospital prescribed for me was giving me migraines from hell. I was in pain and very edgy with everyone. The fact that I was still on sick leave from work wasn't helping. Casey was pretty much the only one I wasn't sending to hell for no reasons. With him I was just bursting into tears often for the slightest reason. I was still feeling guilty as hell.

Most of our friends and coworkers knew about my condition by now, after ending up in the hospital. It's hard to hide it anymore. Most left, but a few stayed by us. Many friends tried to convince Casey to leave me, but it ended up as huge, shouting matches between them and him. I ended up sleeping only 3 hours a night a lot of the time. And in those moments I was once again, alone with my feelings once again, just looking at the moon and stars or at the ceiling in our bedroom, not being able to escape that creeping feeling inside me. Tonight was another one of those nights. A night of squeezing tight the plushy that Casey had gotten me at the hospital, a night of not trying to wake him so he wouldn't be tired like me in the morning.

Medications had been changed one stronger to keep me going. But the side effects were still there. And they were stronger, too. The headaches, the bruises appearing for no reason, the feeling of weakness and loss of muscle control. Add to that was my feelings of inadequacy and the anguish at seeing the pain and worries in the eyes of the guy I love. And now one of the medications I had taken had given me another disease, but that disease was roaming around my liver now. I looked at the sky and asked "why?" realizing I may never get my answer. I was to the point of wanting to scream my frustrations out. I looked at Casey and felt him hug me tightly in his arms. The more I suffered the more I was making him suffer. And hurting him. And I hated myself for that every day more than the last.

Another sad moment of destiny arrived when I was hoping to be reinstated at my job as a teacher. I went to see the Director to tell him I was ready to come back. The look on his face was anything but joy. He said that some parents had learned about my "condition" and the fact that I had a "boyfriend." It seems that they weren't agreeing to have that kind of a teacher for their kids. I tried to argue with him that I was still a good teacher and I would never do anything odd to the kids but apparently the parents had their way. I didn't have the heart to continue arguing with him anymore. I felt defeated and stabbed once again. After a few awkward minutes I left, grabbed my things and walked out with my head down, bobbing like a zombie.

I don't know how many hours I walked through the city streets before I ended up just sitting on the bridge looking at the water and not moving. Through that time I sat numb, while night fell on the city. I think it was close to midnight when I felt from behind two, strong arms hold me as tight as they could while tears fell upon my shoulder. It was Casey. I had worried him again when he heard what happened at school from the Director. Casey thought that he had lost me forever as he searched for me. Now he kept on crying while holding me in his arms, telling me to swear to him that I would never disappear like that again, that if I am feeling sad or anything to just call him even if he is at work. I agreed. But how could I tell him fully how I felt inside?

As the next few weeks passed I rarely got out of our loft. The Most I ever did was to buy groceries or letting Casey drag me out for "sun and fresh air" on his days off. I tried to keep busy by doing my art, and taking care of the loft or pumping iron so I wouldn't turn crazy. But I still refused to venture out, especially on my own. I was too scared that something else would happen. I was to the point of being worried I would lose him, too. I couldn't help but wonder if he shouldn't leave me for someone better, someone that wouldn't be considered a "basket case" In a way I had lost faith in the world. The only person I wanted near me was him. But I was worried that I was wrecking him inside.

Next doctor appointment went terribly wrong. The doctor examining me said that I was so "messed up" and that I should consider therapy and anti-depressant to help stabilize my moodiness. I snapped at him, saying that I refused to take any of those meds because I felt that they would mess me up even further and make my mind worse. Casey put a hand on my shoulder and in five soothing words said, "It will be okay, baby" and then ended up with the three words that kept me warm but at the same time ripped my heart out. Those three words of "I love you". It was amazing and still so surprising for me to comprehend; with the problems I was making him go through, that someone like him could love someone like me. I loved him so much that I would take a bullet for him; that was never in doubt. But even if I was always grateful to have him near me, I still kept wondering why he wanted to deal with all the shit I was bringing in his life.

One day when I was sitting at home, soft music playing while I admired the view through our window, Casey surprised me by coming home in the middle of the day. I got up and told him "Hey babe, why are you home so soon?"

He just walked to me with a big bright, smile and kissed me. Then after a few second he said "I've got a surprise for you, sweetie." He then pulls out plane tickets in first class and tells me "I think we both need a good vacation together, some time to relax together. I know that convention you always wanted to go to is coming in two months."

I am staring at him and he sees that I am about to argue. He kisses me again and then says, "I've already asked your doctor if we should go and he agrees with me. I got a WHOLE month of free time off for us to get ready and leave for some time together. AND I contacted your closest friends to tell them you will finally be there. So please... don't say no."

I looked at him and held him close before I told him "Can I have a day or two to think about it, please?" He looked a bit upset and said, "You don't like my idea? I thought you would enjoy the attention and some time with just us a bit away of our normal lives." I felt another stab in my heart knowing that I hurt him again. "No... it's not that... it's... it's..."

I can't finish my sentence and dart out the door and begin running away through a few streets before I start to walk aimlessly again. I didn't even grab my jacket, my phone or my papers. I just needed to get away. Just so I wouldn't hurt anyone anymore. Especially Casey.

I walked without purpose through the city, my head down and my hands in my pockets, just wondering what to do with my life, wondering how I can live with myself. When I think that all I am good at is hurting him.

As I kept walking through the city I ended up, for whatever reason, at the coffee shop where Casey and I first met. I didn't even have any money on my person to go in about a cup of coffee. So I just sat outside of the coffee shop, remembering the good moments he gave to me, how he changed my life there. And how since then I was ruining his. I looked at the people going in and out of the coffee shop and kept looking at them with envy once again. Just taking me back in that time when I was alone... even if I am not alone now normally... at least.

As I looked at them, I started to wonder if I shouldn't just kill myself. Let Casey be free of his attachments and "obligations" toward me, letting him get his own life without me ruining it. The cold seeps into my bones and I expect rain to fall upon my head to get me drenched then kill me slowly with the wind. I wonder at my options. At this moment I am not even sure I have enough strength to get back home on my own. With no money, I don't even know if the people in the coffee shop would let me call Casey. Maybe this is a Sign from Destiny, to just let myself die away like a shadow in the alleyway. As I look at the people inside "that" coffee shop, I can't help but think about him once again and wish him well... without me.

It is in that moment that I see a cab pulling in front of me, someone jumping out of it to wrap me around in my jacket. I am surprised and look up to see Casey with tears in his eyes again. He hugs me tight with my jacket and his arms, and I hear him say between sobs "I am so sorry babe... I really didn't want you to feel forced... I am so sorry. We don't have to go if you don't feel like it." In reaction I just start kissing him and telling him "Make love to me babe please... make me feel... alive." I see a surprised look on his face as he pulls me in his arms and back to the cab while he whispers to me, "Better wait until we get home if you don't mind, babe." We arrive home and enjoy moments in a way that really makes me feel alive and warm inside. Passionately.

We are both panting afterwards and he is holding me tight against his chest, saying "I had my parents on the phone tonight while I was worried as hell for you, babe." I look down and bury my nose in his chest fur before he adds, "I know you said it wasn't my fault, but well, they would like a chance to meet you at least... even if you don't want to go to the convention."

I look up at him, and can't help but worry for a few minutes, before I tell him "And what if they don't like me? What if it goes even worse? Again." He looks at me with big eyes and just says "I just KNOW they will love you like I do. And if they don't... well I guess I will just keep you and say good bye to them."

"But... I don't want to make your life even worse than I already have."

He then tips my muzzle up to tell me "Babe, the only way you could make it worse is by getting away from me."

He kisses my muzzle deeply before pulling me against him so we, or more like he, can fall asleep. At this point I don't see how I can say no to his request and hurt him more, so I decide to say, "yes." And all I can do is hope that I won't again make it worse for him.

Sleep finally comes for me in the morning while Casey holds me against himself. Whispering to me he says, "I wanted to be sure you wouldn't get up in the middle of the night and don't sleep again." Waking, I lean on him and nuzzle him close while he rubs my back.

"Did you consider my request since yesterday?" I sigh and give him a silent nod.

"Would you agree then?"

I sigh and look up at him slowly before I tell him, "And what if they hate me, babe? What if I hurt you more?"

He just smiles at me once again brightly and says "I told you already, you can only hurt me by leaving me." I hold him tightly and tell him "Okay, I will go with you, babe. I am glad at least your parents accept us as a couple. I just hope they will accept me, too."

He starts rubbing my head gently and says "You know, a friend gave me an advice yesterday."

Looking up I respond, "Another verse of 'leaving me for him?'"

He chuckles and says "No. Actually it's a real advice, for once. He said that, at times, a 'make-over' helps feel better too. So before we go see my parents let's go together and get some new clothes."

I chuckled at that and decided to humor him, especially since what I did yesterday evening to him. We spent the afternoon shopping (which is not already my favorite thing in the world to do), and he ended up trying to create a "brand new me."

At the end of the day I ended up with two new boots instead of shoes, tighter shirts with some designs on them. And the most surprising to me were LEATHER PANTS. I really wasn't expecting that. As I was trying them on he told me "You look so hot in them... it always been one of my kinks, you know. If you decide you agree to go to the convention I bet you will be turning heads." I blushed a bit and couldn't even imagine saying "no" to him after that.

Once we got home he told me "I know you haven't said anything about going to the convention or not, but if we do go they requested that I ask a favor of you. They would like an original from you to show off for the charity. So I was wondering if you would agree to do an erotic nude piece of me?"

He undressed himself and walked over to me. Blushing a bit, I nodded to him as I set up. That night was actually one of the best we had together in awhile. I wasn't thinking about my problems anymore. I was just trying my damn best to do a piece that would do justice to his beauty, inside and out, a way to show the world what a wonderful guy he really is. We talked and laughed like old times, just like nothing ever happened and I hadn't been a problem to him. Around 3 am in the morning I felt pretty proud of myself and he came over to look at it. I was a bit worried he wouldn't like it but he actually held me tight in his arms and told me how much of an amazing artist I was.

Three days later I agreed to go to the convention. We decided to rent a car so we can spend two days at his parent's house before coming back home to get ready for the convention. I wanted to see the friends I held dear to my heart one more time in case something happened to me. And I didn't want to see him cry once again. I wanted him happy. I loved his smile more than my own life.

On the day we were to go see his parents, we got up early in the morning to charge the car before we started on our way. Even though it was only a two-hour drive Casey kept talking to me, taking me down with him through his "memory lane" of where he grew up. When we arrived I was still fidgeting and worrying about how his parents would react to me. He also had a great idea to give me more confidence. "From now on," he said, "I think you should only wear your brand-new clothes." So here I was with brand new boots and leather pants stressing out, as I was about to meet them.

The moment his parents heard the car pull up they both came out of the house to welcome us. There were so happy and overjoyed to see him. When they met me, his dad looked at me with a smile on his face and came over to shake my hand. I felt that his mother was an entirely different matter; it seemed like she had something against me. They had no problem with their son being gay, but having a son who was in an affair with another gay man? We unloaded the car of all our things and went inside to meet his parents and get to know them.

When we got inside the house, they offered us a drink and Casey made me seat right next to him, holding my hand all the while we were talking. They kept asking question about my art, my general well being, and me. Trying to get to know me. But his mother just sat there staring at me, just silent and listening to everything I had to say. When we went to the dinner table, his mother was serving us and all the while she kept on looking at me. The only reason why I didn't freak and run out to the car was because Casey was rubbing his foot on mine as if to let me know he would be there for me through everything in life. And once again that was something that made me happy.

After dinner Casey's dad asked him to go with him to get something in the garage while his mother and I would take care of the dishes. After a few minutes she stops and tells me, "Okay I am sorry. I can't go on like this. I really need to talk to you about this."

"Is there something I did to make you feel uncomfortable?"

"No, no. I just... Well, I know that Casey has found the man that he really wants to spend the rest of his life with."

She stuns me into silence. As I realize that they have has many talks over the phone about me.

"Tell me: How long are you planning to keep hurting my son like that? By not allowing him to share your problems? Don't you see he loves you with all his heart and from what I see of you I now know that he's found a great guy."

"I...I don't quite understand..."

She sighs and then tells me, "Do you remember the day you ran out of the apartment? Or the day after you met your Director at school? My son was out of his mind for concern for you! I don't think I've ever heard him cry that much since he broke his leg as a kid in a biking accident. Honey, my son cares for you with all his heart and he has a big heart, that's for sure. He wants to share your life, and that includes your pain."

She puts a hand on my shoulder and gives me a soft smile. "Our family knows that you are going through a lot, but you do realize that you don't have to go through all of it alone. Casey loves you. He wants to be by your side forever, and that means accepting you *for who you are*, with all your problems. Being in love is relying on each other's shoulders in moments of needs and walking with each other, don't you think? Most families, my husband and I included, have had a tough life. *But we made it through with each other!*"

She then chuckles and says "And I think it shows how much you love him, too. I think you would make a wonderful mate for my son, and a beautiful addition to our family. You're a great guy."

The tears start to build up in my eyes at those words and they fall down my face.

"So you think that I should leave him? That I'd only be a burden?"

She gives a loud gasp at that comment and puts a hand on my cheek to try to stop my tears "No honey, not at all! In fact, the total opposite!"

His mother pulls out a handkerchief to rub my tears away gently as she holds me close. "I fear for my son every day he goes to work because of his job. His situation. But every day I am also thankful that he found someone he cares for so much too. Someone as amazing as you. You give him hope at the end of every day."

"But ma'am... I feel like I keep hurting him more and more every day. Every time a new problem pops out of the blue I know it will hurt him. It hurts me more than going through all of it. I just can't stand it."

She put a finger on my nose and smiles at me.

"It might hurt him but it's all because he loves you, it might be worrying him but that's because he wishes to spend the rest of his life by your side. Just keep it simple for him. Let him love you and love him in return. Face all of the adversities of life side by side. Don't keep it bottled up inside and stop on running from your problems. If he EVER considered that you were ruining his life he would have already left you. Instead he just wants you by his side more and more. That's my son. That's how he is. I know you have as much love as much love inside your heart and soul for him as he has for you." She said.

My tears just flow as she just holds me in her arms, rocking me gently and rubbing the back of my mane. "And he was right, you know," she chuckled, "You have got quite an amazing mane."

I was so surprised by that comment that I chuckle, smiling at her. The time spent with his parents was amazing.

The next day we were walking around their garden when my doctor called my cellphone, asking me if I would come see him tomorrow before we leave for the convention. I was speechless. "What could be wrong now?" I thought. I started bending over with pain in my stomach as it was twisting on himself from stress. Casey saw the distress in my eyes and he took the phone from me to talk to the doctor. Casey's mom came over to soothe my distress. It turns out that the doctor only wanted to talk about the medication for my liver problem and the possible side effects. He said he was sorry to call and make me worry unnecessarily, but he felt that I needed to know as much as possible so I could make my decision while I still had a choice. Panic set in, my heart beating wildly and my stomach cramping. Hanging up the phone, Casey then took me in his arms and brought me to bed, staying by my side. His parents came in to check on me regularly until my panic attack subsided. Casey left to take a quick shower while his mom sat with me.

I looked up at her and said, "I am sorry I am ruining everything once again."

To that she sits next to me on the bed and grins, "Don't make me slap you, mister. Some things are out of your control. Just remember the things we had talked about together, okay? I am sure it'll all get better in time if you two stay side by side. And know you are ALWAYS welcome to stay here with us, if you need time away from the city."

The day after that we were leaving, his mom complimented me on my attire, especially the leather pants. That made me chuckle once again as I thanked her with all my heart.

When we got to the doctor's office I was doing my best to stay calm and thankful that Casey was by my side. His parents had made us promise to keep them informed of the outcome. After several more tests and several hours passing, the doctor came to us and told us that my condition was curable. But the cure that came with a cost. It wasn't a money issue, but rather what side effects I might experience. The doctor informed us that the treatments could last upwards to a year but should be more than enough to get rid of my physical problems forever. But it may make me weak and tired for most of the time. We sat and talked about what I might be able to do in that year, but he couldn't promise me I would manage to do a whole lot. It sounded like I would be nearly back in the same state that got me in the hospital last time and I would be a burden to Casey for most of that year.

When we called Casey's parents about the news his mom right away said that we would either come spend that year with them or that they would come take care of me during that period, so someone would be with me while Casey was at work. Of course I tried to argue with her, but she had made up her mind. She said that there wasn't any other option. And to be careful that the "slap offer" was still on the table, which made Casey raise an eyebrow, not knowing what that meant.

I was really grateful for all of them in my life. His parents were amazing and kind. Casey was fantastic and I couldn't have been luckier than having him as a mate. At this point I was even happier that Casey had offered to go with me to the convention.

Sleep was fleeting during the next three days before our flight. I was using my sleepless nights to do as much art as possible to exhibit at the convention. My art "centerpiece" would be the one I had done for Casey and that the other artworks would be stepping stones leading up to it. I wanted to do my best to make him proud. The tension of those moments gave me cramps and I threw up often. That was worrying him even more but he was supporting me the best that he could.

On the day of our departure we decided to get to the airport early to reduce the possible stress on me. I was glad we had decided to arrive 4 days to the convention before everyone else because the moment we were in the cab going towards the convention hotel my stomach was starting to have stress cramps.

Casey saw this and asked, "Why are you stressing sweetie? It's been okay so far."

"I am worried to disappoint you babe..." I told him.

"You can't disappoint me sweetie." He said. "You are giving all that you have and I will always be proud of you. I'm here for you, you know that."

Arriving at the hotel, Casey took care of everything while I relaxed in bed for the rest of the evening, but not after I managed to convince him to go out for a romantic dinner together.

The next evening I got quite the surprise. Hearing a knock at our hotel room door, I went to open it. My friends had arrived early to spend the last free day with us before the convention started. They all knew about my health and were there by my side like Casey was. And that meant a lot to me. Casey's mother's words and advice were coming true! It was moments like these that I wanted to believe I could live like a normal person, too. That I still had one, small chance in life.

That evening Casey and I even went dancing. It was loud and the crowds were packed but I did my best even if I came back to our room with a headache. Casey's scent next to me helped a lot. It was so nice to be with my friends. They were all so supportive.

Two days after we were installing my art as an exhibit when some other people arrived to install theirs, too. Since I had the best booth in the show we were attracting attention. I was amazed that they hit on Casey while we setting up. He had ignored them at first, but finally started sending them away. It was very clear that they wanted more of Casey than I was willing to share. Their actions were deeply hurting to me I admit, but I couldn't blame him if he would be tempted to go for someone who was healthy and vibrant. But such was my insecurity.

As I was finishing a few minutes later, I asked Casey to hand me a hanger, but he didn't answer. I turned around to find out that he was talking with a big hunk of a Doberman. Convention gossip had it that this Doberman was the assistant for another big shot artist that I took the spotlight from here. Casey seemed to be laughing with the guy and having such a great time. I finished installing the rest of my booth and quietly left without saying anything. On the way to the bar I met other friends and made "small talk", all the while heading towards my destination. The moment I arrived I ordered vodka – not caring if I hadn't got food yet – and feeling my anxiety rise that Casey might be happier with someone else besides me.

After my fourth drink I felt arms circling on my chest as I recognized Casey's scent. He held me for a minute before pulling my face up to meet his.

"I am sorry babe. I really should have been more careful. I should have been helping you."

"Its okay babe, I understand." I said. "I am a basket case after all. I guess it would be normal for you to not want someone dragging you down."

"That's just it. I DON'T want anyone else. I just want you. I sensed he was being friendly just to get dirt on you, sweetheart. When I realized that I grabbed him by the throat and told him to leave us both alone."

I laughed at that and looked at Casey, the best in my life. Going back to the hotel room we had a wild night together. I'm sure it was the alcohol speaking.

The following morning was Show Time. I was The Artist, and in more ways than one and I had to be ready to play the part. Casey told my friends about what happened the day before and they made it a personal responsibility to keep any trouble away from me. It did give me a smile to see them caring for me that way. I set up table with my tools and some material I was offering to sell, while doing small, quick sketches. In the first few hours I barely made two sketches and start to worry as I see the people looking all around. Casey turned to me and said, "The Dealer's Room is coming alive. You know that they start looking around first before they buy."

I did my best to believe in what he said, I really did. But it all clicked when people finally started to line up in front of my stand to get an autograph or a sketch. I was even surprised and felt good that some of them had my very first "illustration book", wanting for me to autograph.

Unfortunately not very far from my table, the Doberman from the day before started to make nasty comments about me. Saying how "people shouldn't even consider touching my products" or shaking my hands in case they'd get "infected." Hearing his comments made and the reactions they got on people's people's faces started to impact me. My stomach started to twist up and tense once again. I started bending over myself and holding my stomach when my friends came over to me. I didn't know where Casey had gone until I heard his voice. He was in the Doberman's face, telling him how much he didn't knew "shit about anything" in life. That the Doberman was just acting like that because he couldn't get Casey in bed. The people around them started laughing and the Doberman bragged that he wouldn't touch someone that went with me, someone that "touched" me. To that Casey laughed and said to him "Want to take me on a fight, you wimp? Maybe you want to test how 'infected' I am??"

At that point the Doberman started to step away, his tail between his legs, unsure of himself as people realized that what he was doing was all for show and braggadocio. He quickly stopped showing off and left. Casey and our friends came to stand right by me, while Casey started massaging my back. He then went into an exclamation of praise: about how proud he was of me to not give up, and all the amazing things I had done in life even in the face of adversity. Then Casey got down on one knee and gave me a long, tender kiss in front of all those people before he gave them a smirk.

They started to laugh and applaud while lining up at my table. And me? Why, I was doing my best to calm down my stomach and do the only job I had come to do.

Later on Casey and I offered everyone to come and share a meal in our hotel room. It was nice to be with people that I loved, and who loved me. It allowed me to spend a relaxing night with my friends and forget my problems for a few hours before I spent a delightful night in the arms of my Casey. And I was grateful to have him near me once again.

The next day went better than the previous one. I made sales, and was actually surprised at the friendliness and kindness of my customers, and for the life of me, I didn't know why. I suspected that most of them knew already about my condition, but didn't care about what others thought.

But then not far from my lunch break, that "big shot artist" himself showed up to tell me off. He started to rant and scream that someone like me shouldn't be allowed in peoples' presence for fear of catching what I had. He started harping about how people could catch my disease by just wanting to shake my hand.

Casey was about to intervene when something just "twisted inside me". I had had enough and got up to face him. I couldn't, no *wouldn't*, let him continue to abuse me in front of everyone. It wasn't right. It wasn't fair. As I went around to the front of my table I saw him making a show of taking a few steps backward to stay away from the "diseased person."

I pointed at him and said, "Don't worry about me. I never even considered getting close enough TO YOU to smell your stink, even less touching you." He seemed shocked and was about to retort when I cut him off and said "Yes I admit it and I won't hide it. I am sick. I 've had it since I am a kid and it has never been my choice. Believe me when I say I would never wish what happened to me anyone... even you."

Sighing, "I had always sworn to myself I would never give it to anyone if I can prevent it, even though that's what the doctor did to me. But I know that some people will never understand. They will live with outdated ideas and past beliefs, ideas that some people think are truth but are completely untrue. They will think that they can catch my disease by shaking my hand or standing too close to me, or even breathing the air that I breathe. Or even sharing the same toilet seat that I been using." Looking around I quietly said, "I even heard some people saying that the silverware and utensils that people like me use should be burned, to obliterate the disease."

I shook my head, breathing deeply before I went on. "But now you using all of people's fears to try to get them running away from people like me. You know, I HATE what I have inside me. There is no other way to say it. It has ruined my life since I was a kid and was the reason why I spent most of my life-avoiding people. To not get hurt once again."

I then point gently toward Casey. "Then I met this wonderful man. He accepted me for who I was, despite my health issues. He has been with me at the hospital and when the meds affected my moods. I As much as hate the disease for myself, I hate myself even more for ruining his life, day by day. Every time we go visit a doctor I am worried he will hear 'one problem too many," leave me on the spot." Tearing up, I added "And I would be lying if said I didn't thought it would be better for him to do so. I often think, 'a wonderful guy like him could do so much better than me. Even his parents have accepted me and made me feel welcomed. I even have friends here present with me, showing their support." As I wave toward my friends present around me.

Tearing and angry, I confront this artist, telling him, "I have been through hell all my life, I've got a tough skin, even if I am emotional. And everyone's love and friendship helped me through this. But if there is ONE thing I can't accept anymore... I WON'T LET YOU DRAG OTHERS INTO THE MUD WITH ME! They don't deserve that. And if Casey were to leave me because of my disease I would be but I would accept it. I keep asking myself if it wouldn't have been a better choice for him, in the end. He has been amazing to me."

I then point at the guy and tell him "And on that matter... I RE-ALLY DON'T NEED YOU TO ADD YOUR SHIT HERE. So if you are 'so scared' of what's going on inside me... THEN STAY AWAY!"

I sit on the floor, realizing that I have spilled my entire life to all those people present.

My friends come to comfort me and I realize that Casey is gone. I tell myself, "That's it. He must have understood that I wouldn't be mad if he left and he did just that..."

My friends try to reassure me that it's probably not that at all. But some people come by my table while I am doing my best concentrating on the sketches asking me why my mate left the dealer suddenly, and in tears I am better leaving my friends to handle those problems. I am too emotional now.

Five hours later the Dealer's Den is about to close, with announcements telling people the programs that will be in that evening's session, and telling them to come back again tomorrow. My friends try to convince to me go eat with them but I am silent, ready to pack away my gear and leave tonight.

A murmur comes from the crowd as people realize that the doors are closed and they aren't allowed to leave. I was surprised that they would not be able to get out but I didn't care. Suddenly a message comes over the intercom for those still in attendance to assemble at table C25 for an important announcement. It is then that I realize that table C25 is my table. We become mobbed, with me trying to hide and get out of the way, but it become apparent to me that escape is not possible.

The crowd starts to part for the Director of the convention.

He gets close to my table, saying, "Ladies and Gentlemen, I have a very important announcement to make. If you wouldn't mind raising your heads and looking at the screens that are surrounding the convention center?"

Asking gently, he says, "Jason would you agree to get up on the other side of the table and stand close to me?"

I swallow loudly and nod, in reaction. I slowly got up, and for the second time in my life, felt like I was heading towards my execution. But this time it will be incredibly public.

Once I am in front of him he thanks me. "Now I really am not the one who wants to tell you something important. It's someone much more important than I."

With a bright smile he then turns and points behind himself and I see Casey there, all sweaty and panting, walking closer to us. From the redness and swollen eyes I know he has been crying too.

But why? Why did Casey come back? Is he going to break up with me in public, in front of this mass of unknown people stuck here for my embarrassment?

Once he is just in front of me, Casey pauses and says, "Jason... I have been listening to what you said to that guy earlier. I finally realized what has been going through your mind all this time and it makes sense. I realize what an idiot I have been. You think I find someone better than you while I actually think there is no chance in hell I can find another guy that would make me feel the way you do. Since that day at the coffee shop you have been in my thoughts day and night. I can't ever consider being away from you, even briefly."

Stepping closer to me he adds "You have been through hell, always alone. And I know why. I've seen how people have treated you most of the time, you need to know that it's over."

Seeing the shocked look on my face, he hurries to add "I don't mean that our relationship is over. What I meant is that you won't have to be alone through it anymore. I want to be by your side, forever."

Blushing, he gets on one knee, and adds, "I even called my parents and they are in total agreement with my decision."

Casey pulls out a box and opens it. Inside contains a simple, laced gold ring.

"Jason, would you marry me?"

I am stunned speechless at that point, gasping for air while the rest of the room pretty much doesn't exist anymore. I look at him, tears falling slowly down my cheeks, "But babe... I will just keep ruining your life... you really don't have to do that.

"He shakes his head and says, "I already told you, babe. You can only ruin my life if you aren't in it. I already called my boss and told him I resign. He understands.

I gasp to hear that and I tell him "But Casey. You loved your job. I ruined that, too?"

He grabs one of my hands and tells me "No babe... you made me realize that I love you more than any job. I want to be with you from now on and go around to all the conventions you feel like going to. Because I love being with you and you are the most important thing in my life. Seeing your smile, feeling your warmth in my arms, hearing your voice, holding your hand, and being your husband. *That* is my new dream, my love."

He then looks closer in my eyes and adds "I will be there for you, helping you along, walking by your side. I will do my damn best to make you smile when you are feeling down. I will be holding your hand through every medication, doctor appointment or hospital stay. I can swear you all this and more."

Hearing all this I start to blush madly as he continues to go on, "My parents already said they would help us, too, and come stay with us if we needed that. And my Mom said that if you dare to say no she will spank your leather ass," he grins.

"If you are sure that is what you want I... I agree to marry you, babe."

To that he smiles widely and starts to cry tears of joy, cameras flashing as he put the ring on my finger, and produces a second, exact copy that I put on his. We share a loving kiss in front of all those people, and we are just so happy to be in each other's arms.

With that, the convention Director motions for the convention servants to bring some drinks to serve people around us.

Hugging him, I just look around us thinking to myself and he says to me "A penny for your thought babe."I quietly speak, "I just can't wait to be over this new medication so that I can marry you, sweetie. You're the most amazing guy I met and I am damn lucky to have you by my side."

Then he laughs and says, "Who said we were waiting for that? We will be starting our move out of the loft as soon as we are back from this convention and then we are going to get married. My mom can't wait to congratulate us and introduce you to all their friends."

I can't help but start laughing at that statement as I realize that his mom is so much like he is.

Once again, as everyone is laughing and cheering around us, I look at the sky. But this time I don't ask anything; I say two simple words "Thank you".

I know that I may have more sleepless nights, more trials and difficulties to go through. But now I've got some real friends and a family that accepts me for who I am. And above all I've got the most amazing guy that I would never have dared to dream about. I will do all I can to keep making them all proud and enjoy every moment. Now I have a reason to fight... a reason to continue.

And that really fills my heart with warmth and hope.

At times you wonder a simple question... should you fight who you are or embrace it.

BORN FROM FLAMES

BY XI "WUFFY" SILVERWIND

Raindrops rapped on the tin roof that late spring afternoon making a husky stir on his bed. Massak's sky blue fur swayed in the draft whipping through the room like the trees in the breeze. He sighed feeling moist air blowing into his fur, soothing his pains. His mind slipped away as the song of the storm hushed his world of worries. Soon the last test would be over, then what? The husky shuddered at the thought and buried his muzzle underneath his pillow trying to muffle it out. The heavy wool blanket itched the husky's nose making him flop on his back. Even if he were assured a position in the civil military, his family would never accept him, unless he could rid himself of what dwelled inside. Massak let out a growl at the thought before ripping a drawer from his nightstand open. In it there was a bottle of vodka that was emptied in a few gulps. Sickened by the by the drink's bite he curled up in his bed until he knocked out.

Gloom turned to dusk making the shadows sprawl out across the dormitory and engulf the sleeping husky in its nightmarish veil. Massak panted heavily with his body hot to the touch. Then everything went cold and the air, once heavy with his own musk, thinned to the scent of a light shower on a lawn. He was back in his hometown, Steeleborough. Massak's stomach churned as he walked the streets. They all knew it he was a monster now. Every furry he passed watched from a distance with their lips locked.

The husky fled down one of the alleys, there was only one place he could go. Rain began to pour from the skies when he finally made to the stairwell of an apartment building. His heart began to race, would she be afraid like the others? Then his only ray of hope, the only one that could make him smile, answered the door. Christine's brown eyes greeted him with warm smile that rivaled her hot orange fur. She fell into Massak's arms, burying herself in the endless sky of his fur. Tears rolled down Christine's muzzle but Massak cooed lapping her tears holding his husky close. It was when Christine looked over his shoulder that Massak could see the two red-coated military men waiting to take him away.

Christine screamed out from her apartment, "I'll wait for you! I'll wait an eternity Massak! I love you."

Suddenly Massak came crashing down to reality when the door to his dormitory slammed. Two white hooves clopped in front of his nose, which twitched from the whisker touching it. The horse snorted a warm breath down the husky's neck but Massak paid no attention and flipped over. With a loud *thud* the horse stomped his hoof down by Massak's ear. The husky launched from the floor and back into bed where he rubbed the bang on his head.

Massak's maw reeked of his favorite drink. The stallion gave a low snort. He hated seeing his friend like this just to deal with life. "Hey! Are you seriously doing this again?" He said in a low grumble.

"Damn it Roman you nearly gave me heart attack and quit trying to take that away from me! I'm not even drunk!" Massak yelled as he reached for his bottle.

"Yes you are and you need to cut it out!" Roman growled yanking the vodka from his paw "Now what's up Massak I know there is something on your mind when you get like this."

Massak growled as the bottle dangled out of his reach in Roman's hoof. "Nothing is wrong, now give it back to me!"

The husky swiped his claw at the glass. Shards scattered across the floorboards and the room filled with the strong stench. Roman folded his ears back in frustration, his green eyes cut through the husky. Massak let out a whimper as the horse yanked on his tail. He forced Massak to look him in the eye.

"Want me to ask again? What is wrong with you?" Roman asked in softer tone that stressed his disappointment.

"I don't know."

"Come on, don't give me that Massak!"

"No that's just it... I don't know... I don't know what will happen after I get out of here."

"Oh."

The two sat on the bed in a dead silence. Massak hunched over to stare through the walls. There was no denying that the fate of both of them ended up in the paws of the civil military's captains. For all they knew either one of them could end up at Xiam's Capitol City or hours away on the Southern Shores. It did not matter though because there was a slim chance his hometown would be taking in another Guardian.

"Bud, you shouldn't worry about these things. I know your mate will be by your side when you get out of here. She has been returning your mail at least." Roman nickered, "Besides you still got to give those captains a show that will knock them from the bleachers."

"Yeah right! Send them flying over the school. That way they all will want me!" The husky chuckled coming to. "Then all I would have to worry about is the groundkeeper coming at me with his rake again."

"Oh I am sure there are heavier, more impressive things you can send flying further than that to have them all begging for you!"

"Like what, this whole school with them in it? Yeah they'd just love me."

"Sure thing bud. Just make sure I am out here before you send this thing into space." Roman gave a whinny before being interrupted by his stomach, "Anyways I wanted to ask you if you wanted to run out into town and grab a bite. It's my treat!"

"Yeah sure thing, just don't expect me to cover the drinks again."

"Nope because you've had enough to drink this evening you silly little husky."

Massak left their room with a smirk and a wagging tail. Roman followed closely behind holding his arm with a sour look on his muzzle.

The town began to bustle with Ministry of Defense cadets as the last of the streetlights flickered on. In ten minutes the streets boomed with music and in another thirty the drunken, testosterone-fueled, twenty-something-year-olds flood the cement. Beating the downpour Roman and Massak grabbed a spot in their favorite club, Skye. The music was loud, the dancers were crazy, and best of all it had Roman's chicken katsu.

The scent of delicious foods were masked under Massak's citrus, floral cologne making everyone turn their heads. A gentle blush hid itself in his fur and brought a smirk on muzzle, which was quickly sealed away by his scruffy hair. Attention was unwanted by the husky even though his look said otherwise. His broad shoulders pressed his biceps in the sleeves of his black button-up shirt. His stonewashed jeans were slim, but not revealing.

Behind him the oceanic scent of Clydesdale wafted in. Roman trotted in wearing nothing more than his favorite pair of cargo shorts. Everyone gawked at the massive stallion stud with his ripped torso, tribal tattoo, and unruly mane. Basking in the limelight he let out a neigh and just as fast as their fame came, it faded away into the sea of neon lights.

After trampling around the dance floor the two managed to grab a table near the bar. Roman's appetite was now dying for dinner, and hot or not, there was no holding him back from the crispy bite of that chicken. Soon a raccoon dog waiter came up the two awaiting their orders.

"What'll ya have tonight boys?" He asked placing the flatware down.

"Oh I dunno I think I will just stick with the house sake and the two orders of the chicken katsu." Roman replied.

The waiter's eyes grew wide behind his pad of paper while he wrote down the order. Then he finally glimpsed at the stallion laughing above him, and slapped his forehead in embarrassment. "Oh I am sorry about. Wasn't expecting a big guy like you tonight." He said and turned to Massak who was almost as tall, "Make that two big guys tonight!"

Roman playfully popped his knuckles at the table and sputtered. "Hey what is that supposed to mean bud? Are you trying to call us fat?" He exclaimed.

"No! No! Not at all. Just complementing you is all!"

"Oh I bet so. I see your game, calling us fat then trying to flatter us."

The raccoon dog found himself trapped under the stallion's arm in a headlock. Roman chuckled looking down at his catch. The waiter joined him with an uncomfortable laugh while his eyes begged to be saved.

Sunken in his seat and hiding his face, Massak watched the two with a blush on his muzzle. He was so red that it almost looked like the fur on his face had been dyed earlier, but after clearing his throat the timid cuteness was gone. His paw banged on the table making the lights sway above them. "Okay you two settle down!" Massak exclaimed, freeing the raccoon dog from his awkward prison, "Anyways I was thinking about having some pad thai, little guy. Oh and would you please make me a cocktail, you know a Karma."

"No. Actually I don't know sir. B-but I am sure we can make it for you." The waiter gulped.

"It's a double shot of vodka shaken with apple juice and some strawberry syrup." Massak explained with his paw on the raccoon dog's shoulder, "And don't be afraid of me, okay? I am not as goofy as that one over here."

In a blink of an eye the waiter fled behind the bar without even a nod. A few strands of his fur twirled in the wind, slowly floating to the floor before being wafted back up by the raccoon dog with their drinks. Nervously he watched as Massak took a slip from the cocktail glass. The drink burned Massak's lips, it was a bit stronger than the ones he mixed up, but he could sense the fear coming from above the table. Two fangs peered from under the husky's lips after downing the entire glass. Before the waiter could even let out a grateful sigh Roman winked, smacking him on the butt. In another flash the waiter disappeared behind the bar.

"Great, just great Roman you traumatized him so much he isn't coming back!" Massak snarled.

"Oh what! I was being playful." Roman snorted. "Besides I know the little guy loved it, did you see the way he was looking at me in that headlock?"

Massak scowled across the table hearing that lie. Roman just knew how to get under his fur because it was all done just to get him to blush. "He looked more like a deer stuck in the headlights, not some-one that wanted to be teased endlessly by a big goof of a stallion!"

"Reminds me of someone else I used to know. You know, some-one very blue and shy." Roman grinned scooting closer to Massak. He hated it when that husky wore his mask. If he would just lighten up like back at the school maybe things would be different. Maybe picking on others wasn't the right approach though. Grabbing the husky in his arms the stallion squeezed tight and nibbled on one of his ears.

"Not now Roman!" Massak started to giggle. A warm blush final-ly worked its way on to his muzzle. He tried poking at the horse's one weakness, his side, but froze when he saw a white-tailed stag staring at them with that famous dazed look. Embarrassed the two of them went back to their seats with their ears folded back.

"Alright now I feel like an ass..."

"Makes two of us."

The two sat silently waiting for the time to pass. Stares shot across the room and pierced their fur in a burning sting. Then when the moment was up everything returned to the drunken blur of the nightlife. Still Massak retreated behind a tuft of his scruffy blue hair, red hot from the shame. Not even Roman could stop him from drowning the fire under double-shot in his glass. Before he order another, the server cam rushing out with their dinner.

The spicy steam of his pad thai brought drool to his muzzle, leaving the waiter just enough time to slip away from the husky's iron grip. He grabbed his fork in paw and shoveled the savory noodles down. Roman had not had a bite of chicken and Massak was nearly finished with his plate. The horse smiled from across the table. Now *that* was the husky he knew!

"Wow was that all it takes you to get loosened up? Some chicken? Or is that just the chili powder getting into your head?" Roman said.

Massak's ears perked and his head shot up from the table. One thin noodle dangled from the tip of his whiskers. Smudging a napkin across his face, the husky stared back at the horse, realizing that again he let his guard down. He said slyly, "No no! That is just the beast coming out in me. You know pony, I am just a wolf after all."

"Oh sure mister fox. I am sure someone as cunning and suave as yourself can avoid being seen eating like a werewolf." Roman sighed with smile, "Or are you sure it wasn't just the real you showing up?"

"Nope, definitely not the real me showing up! Just the beast."

"Oh okay I see. Then the beast would not mind if a horse shouted across the room about how adorable the beast is.

"No, he would not mind, but he would have a full stomach of one pestering stallion, dipped in katsu sauce of course."

Roman punched the husky on his shoulder and sputtered." Then do you mind lightening up you goof? You know I know that that is the real you and so does everyone else now."

"Fine..." Massak mumbled under his breath trying not to look at anyone.

"Look I don't know what you have to be shy about when you are as amazing as you are... well except when you are hungry... but seriously just try to have some fun. Who cares if they think you are..."

"Gay... like you Roman."

The stallion bowed his head, the way Massak said it just cut deep. "You make it sound like it's so horrible." Roman sighed.

Now Massak really screwed up. It took a lot to take the cheer away from a stallion with such a happy-go-lucky attitude. He folded his back and let the warm touch of his paw do most of the talking. "It's not horrible at all bud," Massak paused, "And you know that doesn't change how you are as a furry. I just can't take being called another name, when I have been called them all my life."

"So, you think it is any different for me?" Roman snorted, "Everyday cubs would call me weird because of what is inside of me, just like you, and then when I came out in high school it got worse. But you know what it never broke me..."

"That's why you are much stronger than me... Just please don't let how I say something get to you... We'll still be friends no matter what."

Roman smirked under his forelock before grabbing the husky's paw in a tight squeeze and nodding once. He wanted to give the husky a hug just to seal the deal but he knew that would only cause Massak to sink away once again. Leaning into Massak's ear, he whispered, "Just watch your back though when we get back to the dorm because I am going to squeeze you tight, bud."

Wagging his tail, Massak threw his arms around the stallion's chest and squeezed tight. He did not care who saw it this time! Roman's bones popped under the husky's massive muscles as he tried wriggling one of his arms free from the grasp. Stuck the horse banged his hooves on the floor. Massak eased up his grip to whisper, "You mean like that?"

"Yeah like that! Now who are you and what have you done with Massak?"

"I told you I was the beast."

Massak's muzzle was bright red again as he struggled to make a low growl. Did he really just do that in public? For once he actually felt free, and no one was staring, or mumbling under their breath. Everything was just¬¬— normal. Maybe it was just the drinks finally starting to get to him. Nah that couldn't be it because even that can't get him to bust out the happy-husky-mega-squeeze, at least not while furries were around. That's it! It was that thing he heard others talking about, what was it though, outgoing? Well, whatever it was it sure felt amazing.

"Yeah right a beast of blushes. We better get back home, cause I can already tell you are plastered doing that." Roman chuckled throwing his arm over the husky's shoulder.

"Pfft for once it isn't the alcohol, I am not even sure what came over me." Massak replied, "But hey, you don't see me running for the door now do you?"

"No, that is what scares me and makes me want to start heading that direction."

"Oh what cause I can squeeze you again?"

"No, because you are embarrassing me!"

Roman quickly ruffled the husky's hair and shot up form his chair to dart to the bar. Flustered he reached for the horse's tail, yanking him back to the table with a metallic screech coming from his shoes. The stallion nickered, he tried pulling away, but it was no use that dog was like boulder. The husky blew the fur out of his muzzle as he leaned in close to an ear. "Seems like it is payback time huh?"

With a jerk of his arm the stallion threw the husky into a squeeze, while whinnying loud enough so that the whole club would look. Only a few turned their heads but Massak could not see a thing under the feathered fur on Roman's forearm. The husky grabbed the horse's paw with his iron grip and twisted him around so that he would land in a headlock. By now, several tables had gotten up to watch the show. Massak's cold nose pressed on the stallion's neck, making his brown pelt twitch with the gentle tickle of his whiskers. For once the horse was the one sweating as the crowd started to mumble under the blasting music. "Want me to give them more to see?" Massak whispered, putting his paw on the stallion's belt.

"You wouldn't—" Roman shouted but he could not finish in time. His shorts were already on the floor, which made the club roar seeing his lavender boxer-briefs. For a minute it was almost like a storm went off in the dinning room because the room flickered with camera flashes capturing the moment. Blinded and defeated, Roman sucked up his shame. The ladies screamed as he flexed his pecs and posed for another round of photos. Damn he always knew how to turn things around in his favor. Sharing the spotlight, the stallion tugged Massak forward by his tail and shouted.

"Show 'em the gun show bud!"

The sleeves exploded off his biceps in ribbons of mangled cloth His light blue fur was pressed tight as his arms bulged. His height only stressed the raw power surging through his body, making the seams of new vest tear away. Massak's ears stung with the shouts of his now-adoring "fans". Without turning a different shade, he changed his pose to show off all the pain-staking work put into his six-pack. There was only thing to say about the husky so cool in color, he was hot, hotter than he could ever imagine

Nearly everyone had flocked to the two, whistling for more as the half-naked husky worked his muscles even more. Ladies cheered behind their cell phones but over the crowd was an outsider, sailing on the sea of raging estrogen. Massak caught a glimpse of a set of antlers drifting around him, as if circling him like prey. Then they stopped. Two hoofed hands held up a cell phone, illuminating the deer's white muzzle in a soft glow. Massak froze mid-pose, watching that camera snap a photo, and with a churn of his stomach the canine was sick.

What had he just done? It was one thing to put on a show but not for this guy, especially when he ran into him twice. It all seemed too weird, no gay guys ever hung out at his place, and the time was getting closer for graduation. That is when it dawned on him. That deer could be working for one of the Colonels, scouting out the school before they are allowed to arrive searching for students' weakness so that they could throw it into the trails.

Massak tapped the stallion on his shoulder. The girls let out a collective aw as the stallion returned his shorts to his waist. He snorted while turning to Massak, "What is it now!"

The husky nudged his head over to the antlers and whispered, "Just keep your guard up. I have a feeling that guy is scouting us out for next weekend."

"What that deer?" Roman asked, trying to catch glimpse over the last remaining females wanting a picture. "Nah it couldn't be, could it?"

"What kind of stag just walks up here nonchalantly, takes photo, and just wonders off back on to the dance floor?"

"Yeah you are right Massak, that is very weird. You think we should go back?"

"No, I want to see what he is up to or at least see if I can find out who he is sending those photos to." For a second the deer made eye contact the two and his muzzle shifted, he looked worried. His antler grazed one of the male wolves on the shoulder, gashing the wolf's skin, and making the deer run off to the deejay.

"Well, he is sneaking off to the dance floor." Roman asked in a whisper, "You think I should go over there and ask him to dance?"

"No, that would be too direct. He has already knows we have seen him. You should just sneak up on him, you know dance around and try to catch him off guard." Massak explained.

"Woah wait! You want me to go alone?"

"Well yeah..."

"Don't you think it would look strange being a lonely stallion dancing around? Especially when that guy knows we are probably friends or something."

"I can't dance..."

"Oh no! Now is not the time for you to have two left feet. You want to know what he is up to you get out there and shake your ass with me. I don't care how gay you think you look either!" Roman exclaimed tugging the husky by his tail. Massak's toenails scraped against the wooden floor as he was dragged out with the horse.

"But..."

The husky was not lying. He really did not know how to dance. The electronic music was not like anything he heard before on the radio. He was lost between the loud booms of the bass and the robotic voice repeating the same words over and over.

Roman had no trouble moving his hips to the song in way that made him blend in. The husky tried following his lead but he could not match the music making his moves awkward. It was not until the song changed that he got down rhythm that could fit in with rest. He scanned the room beneath the flashing lights. Then the music paused and the lights went off. When the song picked up again, the lights did not. Glows sticks swung wildly in the blackness and the deer was lost.

Massak growled trying to shuffle forward through the furries to find him. Just as he went to take a step, a Clydesdale's hoof stomped in front of him. Roman grinned while he ground his crotch on the husky's abs. Snarling, Massak grabbed the horse's waist and gave it a squeeze but Roman did not stop. He merely let out a whinny while bucking harder with his hips. In one thrust Massak was knocked off to the side and there the deer was with his antlers lit up like a neon tree, in the thick of it all. Two hooves rubbed his back to smear some of the green goo into fur. Roman winked, "You are gonna have to make it hot bud if you want to get to him."

"Just be happy the lights are out!" Massak sneered. He took some of the glow-sticks that Roman managed to nick. *Snap!* Neon ooze splattered against his chest, outlining his abs in a toxic glow. Even his happy trail was matted in a green mess.

Once again the husky struggled to get into the beat but it did not matter. He started to pant working his body under all the fur. Then finally, following Roman's lead, the two penetrated the pack. Massak's heart began to pound in his chest. He was way out of his comfort zone brushing against strangers and having them grind back on his body. Between flashes of the strobe lights a few of the furries turned to see the hunky husky behind them. He was so embarrassed when a male German shepherd turned around, but instead of balling up his fist the dog went about dancing, even as to go so far as to tuck his tail between the husky's legs.

Nervously Massak bucked his hips, playing into the dog's game, while hiding his face under the luminescent streaks of his hair. Out the corner of his eye, he saw a female husky, probably the German shepherd's mate. She watched her mate with hunger as if asking for more. Struggling to let out a murr, Massak moved forward to the husky, leaving the mate to deal wit Roman. She ran her paws up his chest. He shivered while forcing out wide grin that told her to keep going. That was when her paw changed direction. The husky worked her way under the waistband but before she could feel a thing a white hoof stopped it. Roman nodded in disappoint at the husky, sending her and her mate on their way. However, Massak stood there paralyzed. Never in his life would he have expected anyone to do *that* to him.

Nudging the husky with his nose, Roman pointed to a pack of does surrounding the stag. The two penetrated the pack with a tap on a doe's shoulder. They all squealed seeing the two burly furries ready to dance. Coolly Roman pointed to the stag, making a low growl that pulled him from his friends. The stag was blushing wildly while he fell into the stallion's chest.

Massak felt a tug on his tail and a hoofed paw slip into his back pocket. Damn horse, now was not the time to tease him, the husky thought, but then he could see what Roman was doing. The screen on the stag's phone barely lit his pocket so that it could be seen. Massak gulped going forward to stick his paw down there to fish it out. Clumsily the husky brushed his paw against the stag's tail, quickly alerting him to his presence. Even beneath the curtain of darkness the husky could tell he was ready to flee because of the hooves clopping feverishly away into Roman's body. Just as Massak went to rip the phone away the heavy techno music stopped and the lights were thrown on. There the stag was trembling violently against Roman's hip, the poor guy must have scared to death of him.

Massak folded his ears back feeling the stag's fear. The does watched out of curiosity as the husky softly padded forward with a small grin on his muzzle. With a nod of the head and a paw of the shoulder, the three walked away from the dance floor, leaving a group of does giggling at the lucky stag.

"Sorry to scare you like that, but we decided to stalk you back tonight." Massak said, finally being heard over the dull roar of the music.

"Uh... I didn't mean to be a creep like that... I just wasn't expecting to find anyone like you here." The deer explained while he nervously played with his thumbs, "If I knew you guys were wanting to talk to me I wouldn't have done it."

"Oh it's nothing, and just ignore the blue husky touching your butt. He is really shy once you turn the lights on and get a good look at him." Roman nickered, making Massak light up red, "See! Very very shy."

"Hehe I see. So why is it that you were trying to steal my phone? Are you trying to secretly put your number in there or something? The stag chuckled.

"No! But the way you were lurking about made us think you were someone else." Roman said, "You see it graduation time for the Ministry of Defense students and you know what that means?"

The deer scratched his head and replied, "Ah I think I remember my friends saying something about it last year. Some of the higher-ups in the military and make you guys perform at our college's stadium."

"Uh huh that is exactly it!" Massak exclaimed, "And well w thought you were one of the Colonel's scouts. You know trying to weed out us out before the trails are set to take place. Not that it matters for me and him, just well we don't want to be sent to the Southern Shores if we don't have to."

"Well why doesn't it matter? Can you not be chosen to graduate if they see your skills aren't ready?" The deer asked, "Unless you two are a couple of the guardians?" His voice seemed to trail of into a slow realization. Then without even the faintest warning he let out a squeal that could rival his female friends. "Oh my! I have never been so close to a guardian before! I have only seen them on TV. What is it that you do?"

Without a word the two of the two of them pressed a finger to their grinning muzzles. It was against code to demonstrate their powers when they were not needed, but since the guy seemed so into the idea then surely just one little trick wouldn't hurt, at least on one conditions. The husky winked over at the stallion. "Oh I am sure we can show you what we do but no pictures." Massak said holding out his paw.

"And you must tell us what you were thinking we were in the first place!" Roman exclaimed as he threw himself between the two, "I am sure that Massak is very curious of *that* too!" The stallion had that look on his muzzle that could only mean that he was up to no good, but who was this joke on and what of?

The stag nodded handing over his phone to Massak who was now searching the room frantically. It had been forever since anyone, beside Roman, had seen him in action. Maybe it was the overwhelming fear of someone watching him, judging him, and his true self that made the husky resist. Then maybe it was the fact that there was nothing around for him to show off with or at least not anything big like he was used to. "Hey do either of you have a half-buck I can use?" He asked.

Roman fished around his pocket finding a few coins that he handed over to the husky. Massak smirked, pressing the metal disc flat into his paw, removing all the engraving. "Also I hope you are in the mood for some taffy!" He said stretching the metal out into a thin, silver ribbon that hung an arms length before breaking. The deer was shocked to find that it really was metal that Massak was working with as examined the ribbon. For an added bonus the husky used his lesser ability to freeze the strips cold enough to make it brittle. Even Roman tilted his head as he saw the small ice crystals growing in size. In a snap of the fingers the metal exploded into shards that littered the wooden floor.

"Wow! So that must mean you have some super strength and magic in you!" The deer exclaimed.

"Well the super strength is the main thing. I picked up magic while studying at the teachers' college many years ago. It was funny, he was a small timid wolf kind of like you that bargained to teach me a few tricks if I agreed to help him in the gym." Massak chuckled, "I had him turned into a brute by the end of the semester."

"So wait you are a teacher, and a body builder, and a drafted member of the CM?" The deer asked, confused at the husky's history.

"I am more the last of those two things now. My high school teaching days are long over." Massak sighed, "But hey what can I do? I am a guardian after all."

"Good thing I wasn't in your classes then. I would have been too afraid of getting crushed in your arms if I did bad on exam."

Massak almost started to blush, why was it everyone thought of him as the big bad wolf? Least he could d was play it up now. "Oh there were only, I think six crushings, maybe seven." Massak said trying to keep straight face, "But I don't think would have liked my classes too much anyways. Advanced organic chemistry one and two was not something most of the students took at my school, let alone survive because their body builder teacher."

"You are one smart furry if you taught that human science stuff." Said the stag now turning his attention to the stallion. "What about you big guy? Are you going to pick up the bar and toss it through the wall."

"Not exactly, the bar but maybe a few stools. I really leave the demolition to the cute innocent husky, that way no one gets exiled to the island." Roman chuckled, "But thanks for the compliment thinking I am stronger than him."

Massak wagged his tail as the stallion scratched a his mane so that he could hide the pink tint on his muzzle. Was the only thing that could break the stallion's cockiness really as easy as saying a few nice words? "Heh I think you broke him little guy." He said slapping the horse on his back, "Go on Roman, he is waiting."

"Hold on! I am thinking of something. You got to remember my powers aren't as showy as yours are, especially if you blink." Roman said, "Wait you live at the University right, the one on the other side of town?"

"Yeah but—"

"And your laptop is in there right? Here give me the keys to your dorm and I will go fletch it for you."

"But how do I know you won't come stalk in the middle of the night when I am alone?" The stag hinted.

"Oh trust me there are other ways of getting you alone!" Roman snorted playfully, "Now can I just borrow your keys for a minute? I promise I won't be in the bushes tomorrow ready to pounce you after classes."

"Alright here they are, room twenty-six in the Lioner Hall."

In a great gust of wind the stallion vanished. Dancers were left dumbfounded, thinking that a storm had whipped through the entrance of the place. Even the stag stood there confused as he watched the husky take out his watch. "Just give him five more seconds and I am sure he will be back. Three... two... one..."

In the same gust of wind the stallion was back with a laptop and a pair of boxers in his paw. "Oh what a cute pair of pink Silverwinds I found laying around." Roman said stretching the underwear out, "A size thirty? Wow you really are a tiny stag. Oh yeah your laptop, it's right here too."

The deer blushed wildly having his underwear shown off like a flag in the wind. Roman whinnied teasing him for a few jumps before looping the boxers on his antlers. "At this point I would rather have been crushed by the husky. Anyways you can either teleport or run really fast I take it?"

"Nah my ability is to tease cute guys like you into giving me the keys to their rooms so that I can do naughty things." Roman growled.

"Heh sure but that still didn't answer my question. Are you running or is it some sort of powerful magic you are using?"

Roman was a little upset he could not muster even a smile out the stag. "Fine then. Since I guess you like the idea of me being in your bedroom then I won't be needing these." He said chucking the keys towards the ceiling, and disappearing from sight. Yet instead of *clang* hitting the ceiling the stallion dangled from the steel rafters with the keys on one finger. The air whirled around the two as Roman made his landing and placed the key ring on another antler. "And to answer your question it's running mixed with some high speed parkour. Not teleporting." He sputtered.

"You two make an awesome duo! Can I just get one pic with the two of you? Without being a creep this time."

"Not uh, remember you have to keep up your end of the bargain? Go on tell the big mean husky why you originally came up to us."

Massak tilted his head watching the deer blush with his ears folded. Then it hit him like sack of bricks, the one thing he tried to avoid conveying all night was what that stag must be. The deer was gay. It all made sense now! That damn Roman had set the husky up this entire time with all the dancing and flexing. The stallion winked as he rubbed at Massak's shoulder, probably trying to ease some of the tension before being popped in the shoulder.

"Well the truth of it all you guys... is that I am gay and well when I saw you two messing around in the dining room... I thought that maybe you two were too." The stag folded his ears admitting, "I thought I would come join you but the way that husky looked at me I thought he was going to kill me I sat in. I just didn't want to be with all my female friends as they swooned over some meat-headed, homophobic idiots."

Ashamed of himself, Massak padded forward and wrapped the deer in his arms for a hug. As much of a shock it was at first, it did not sting as much as the fact that he scared another furry into running away from him. That is all furries did when the found out his powers, thinking of him a monster, but not anymore, not for this furry. Even if his sexuality looked iffy to all those around him, Massak murred softly holding him for a few seconds longer.

Massak explained. "I am sorry if I came off to you like that. I just am not used to anyone being brave enough to come up to me like that... I am just so used to furries seeing me as some rabid wolf and I didn't want to give them another reason to stare by acting gay."

"So, you mean you are not..."

"No, no I am not... I am sorry. But hey at least this stud is."

"Oh great!" The stag exaggerated while rolling his eyes, "Well that is shame because you two would make one hot couple together. Are you sure you aren't lying to me?"

"You know if I didn't like breathing so much I would tell you that he is lying." Roman laughed, pulling the husky into a headlock. "Besides even if he was do you think a stallion like me would be with him? Pfft yeah right."

"Yeah you are right this husky is *way* too hot for you."

"Damn you cut me deep bro, really really deep."

"Heh I know but you tease your friend too much. I thought it would be nice if I fought back for the big bad wolf. Anyways guys can I get a photo before you two vanish off into the night?"

"Sure thing bud."

The two posed like before with their muscles bulging in the remainder of their clothes. The deer was stuck in the middle, flexing his arms trying to match the studs behind him. In one last flash of the night the picture was taken, and the three parted ways. Massak and Roman made their way outside the club, the streets had finally started to ease up, making the town mostly silent amongst the booming basses locked in the clubs. The stallion trotted alongside Massak, circling him with a cheesy grin on his muzzle.

"Seems like the husky has a few tricks up his sleeves. I really was not expecting you to hug the guy after he came out to you. Maybe you really aren't such a hard ass when it comes down to it." Roman whinnied loudly in Massak's ear. The husky rolled his eyes not saying a word. He tried pushing the stallion out of the way but it was no use. By the time his blue paw touched the stallion's chest, he was scooped up, and being nibbled on. The whiskers on Roman's snout made him wriggle in laughter.

"Okay! Okay! The beast is a big softie at times." Massak panted as he tried breaking free, "But only at times! The rest of the time he will bite your head off, if you keep nibbling his neck with your big horse teeth."

"Oh well I can live without it!" Roman chuckled, "I am so proud of you bud, you broke out of your little box tonight. I knew I could get you out!"

Then a shrill scream pierced the night sky. It echoed off the brick walls and hit the two like a train. Some one was in trouble! Without even thinking Roman dashed to a nearby rooftop with Massak still in his grasp. Shaken, the husky stumbled to his paws still dizzy from the trip. Below them were three burly wolves teaming up against a lone furry that was cowering on the ground. In the distance was the same group of does watching in horror. The wolves shifted around giving them a glimpse of a bloody stag on the concrete.

"Get up you fag!" One of the wolves snarled.

Buckling under the weight of his own body, the deer weakly picked himself up to his knees when another wolf swung his leg to kick him in the head, with a *crack*! It wasn't the deer's antler's cracking together though, It was the wolf's bones being crushed under a hoof.

"You leave him alone you assholes!" Massak snarled.

The wolf whined helplessly under the horseshoe and the others came charging. Massak cracked his knuckle and wound up a swing to one of the wolf's gut. His punch landed with a crack of thunder that shook many of the nearby windows. Gasping for air the wolf fell to the ground clutching his stomach. The last of the wolves tore into Massak's shoulder with their maw. The husky reacted swiping at the canine with his claws. His wrist caught the wolf on the chest and sent him skidding against the ground in a dust cloud. Roman quickly rounded the three up in a pile while Massak went to the stag's aid. As he leant to check on the deer's vitals, he felt a weak kiss at his cheek.

"Thank you." The stag said weakly before collapsing into the husky's arms.

Massak held the stag in his arms watching his breathing, worried that at any moment it might stop. One by one the does ran to their fallen friend. Just as fearful as the husky they fell to their knees and waited for help to arrive. Then down at one end of the alleyway a black car pulled up. Its tinted kept the occupants hidden but they all sighed in relief when four scarlet suited furries came running to control the situation. In a matter of minutes an ambulance came along with several squad cars. The civil military swept the drunken frat wolves away into the night while the stag was being laid out on the stretcher.

Massak ran to the paramedic. "Will he be alright?"

The ram nodded, "Yes sir he should be fine. Just don't worry the healers should have him roaming the streets in the morning."

The meal door of slammed shut and, like the wolves the stag was whisked away into town. Much to their surprise a member of the car walked to them. He too was a stag, but was much more bulky than the one they saved. Medals clanged on his chest as he walked forward with a smirk. The leaves on the brim of his kepi laced it in gold, which made him, without a doubt, one of the visiting Colonels. All of them, including the soldiers that accompanied him in the car stood steadfast and saluted.

"At ease soldiers!" The elk demanded.

"Yes sir Colonel Buchanan!" The all shouted, except for Massak and Roman who hadn't been able to see his name tag.

"You two must be the guardians we all came to see. I must say that was quiet heroic of you both coming to that boy's help like that." He said, "Very noble stuff you two."

The two of them stood there unsure of what to say. Both of the knew the amount of force was excessive but it wasn't like they were officially apart of military yet. The elk shook his head looking at the two and he extended his paw. "What a shame those guys just couldn't play nice in the first place and since I can tell by the silence you two must be exceptionally tired." Colonel Buchanan said, "Come on now! Hop in the car and we will drop you off at the academy. Oh and Maurice could you please hand them one of the coats from the trunk, a chill is starting to whip through the air."

These next few seconds would be forever etched in his memory. The warm wool coat clasped tightly against his chest, it was an officer's uniform still bare for a new cadet. For the first time in his life, he had used hi powers for good, and there he stood, beneath the streetlight, as handsome as ever, in the same scarlet suit shining bright like a diamond.

*One simple decision can also very simply change
everything following it... even for others than yourself...*

LIFE CHOICES

BY N. "KARMAKAT" FRANZETTI

Tyron:

Here I am once again. Went to a jogging at 4 Am in the very early morning dew, hoping to relax and now I am back at our kitchen table working on my weapons again. Everyday it's the same problem with my lack of sleep, the problem dealing with what goes to my mind. The only moments I calm down is when I work on my weapons, when I bury myself into work... or best when he is near me. But I can't wake him up at 3 Am every morning just for a selfish reason of wanting him near me so I can feel better.

As I take my first weapon apart on the kitchen table to clean it as I do nearly every day, I start thinking about the past... about how we met. I was five years old, left in front of the orphanage since I was a baby. I was always closed on myself; barely talking with anyone to the point they thought I had a mental problem. My problem was... I didn't care for anyone in the world. I was a lonely lion in my own little world not caring to spend time with anyone just look at the stars and nature. Then one morning, the day they called "my birthday", because it was the day they found me, that new baby was deposited in front of the orphanage too. He was a hybrid of a fox and a wolf and like me he had nobody. That day everyone was trying to find me for my birthday, but I was with him. I was the one that heard him on our front gate, when they found me I was holding him in my arms and rocking him gently while singing the lullabies they kept singing to all the other kids.

They looked at me like I had just had kittens in front of them I swear; just because I had found someone I was acting "normally" with. I was taking care of him and holding him against me, and this was the start of a different situation for me at that point. I had been given the name Tyron Wilson and from that moment I kept taking care of him. First night I even made them freak out when they couldn't find him in his bed, until they found me holding him against me in my bed both sound asleep. Then they realized that if I wasn't taking care of him and having him near me at night he wouldn't stop crying and screaming his little lungs off. So they finally gave up and let me take care of him. When it was time for him to start going to school they had given him the name Vincent Turner and he was coming with me holding my hand every day, I wouldn't have had it another way. When someone tried to bully him they had to deal with me, and I ended up in the principal office because they kept saying "I wasn't feeling my strength" and sending the kids to the nurse. When he was sick I was spending the whole night by his side taking care of him. And even our "birthdays" were together since it was the day we got discovered. With him I had found a reason to act social.

I had even joined judo classes and competitions to protect him better; he had found his pleasure in lab work and basketball. Every time one of us was in a competition the other was there to cheer him on as loud as possible. But when I had my diploma the orphanage couldn't get me any further at school, and I couldn't stay with them either being too old. I didn't want to go without him, but without a job by myself I couldn't even ask them to let me adopt him. That day I took my decision, I would use those five years of difference between us to make a good situation for us so I can take good care of him and allow him to get his degrees in whatever school he will want. I knew his grades would be there, what he needed is someone able to support him as a "family", so I did the only thing I could. I joined the navy with a three years contract, knowing they would train me and teach me all kind of stuff. That day he cried so badly I felt my heart break, but I was staying strong in front of him... I had to. We promised to keep in contact as often as possible by mail and phone calls every times I could, and I went in the bus. I don't think I cried that much in my life but I wanted to do this for him. When I arrived there my superior had saw me in competitions, he made me pass some shooting tests and fight with the army knife right away. Finding out I was quite a marksman they enrolled me right away in an assault battalion and trained me with sniper rifles. Six months later I was sent to my first war, I had to kill so much people so I could survive and see him again that I felt like my body was becoming ice. The only moments that ice was melting was when I had a letter from him or I was able to hear his voice. I remember even the nickname the rest of my squadron had given me "ICE BULLET", saying because I was acting like full ice when I had a mission or someone to kill even if I was reliable to protect their back. At times an enemy was getting close enough to me thinking that I was just good with my rifle but was ending up meeting my knife. I had so much blood in my hands I never thought I could wash it away, but I wanted to survive and get a good job after those three years to take care of him, and no one would stand in my way for that.

When the three years were finally done the navy asked me if I wanted to renew and I told them no, that I had still something to do outside of here. They still gave me letters of recommendations, that plus my medals, allowed me to join the police and make inspector in a year and half. I kept saving all the money I could, do placements and when the time was right I bought us an apartment on top of a bakery in a nice suburb, with a giant balcony and two bedrooms. Only one thing was missing: Vincent.

The day of his graduation I had taken the week off and was there to surprise him. He really had grown up, and was letting his head fur grow longer to look a bit like a lion. He was graduating with honors and the moment they called his named, I stood up and when he received his paper I took pictures discretely, then waited for him as he came outside. When he passed the door I gave a big roar and he turned his head so fast I was worried he would get a whiplash. When he saw me he started crying and ran into my arms. I had changed a lot too, I had scars physical and emotional, but he was still the only one that could make me smile like that. And finally he was moving with me and able to go on a double degree of biology and chemistry.

As I finish reassembling my sniper rifle and putting it back in his case, I think about the fact that it's already two years that we moved in together. During my days I was only smiling when I was with him, and it still goes one. I don't even have any love interest, all I care is to give him a good life and I work my tail off for that, solving cases after cases, because I want him to go on. To my point of view he is perfect; he is the only one that can melt the "ICE BULLET". Even after all those years that nickname still stuck with me, and my colleagues were calling me "Ice" more often than Tyron at this point. Even the swat team was calling me at times if they needed sniper support, I was agreeing only because of the extra money given in those situations so I could save for him. Yep all I do is for him because he is the one that keeps me warm and going. He was my anchor and without him I couldn't go on, I was sure of that since years. Even if now I come with a "package" since my three years in the navy, but we weren't really talking about that ever, he just knew I was there mostly.

After checking my gun and knife I decide to get up and prepare breakfast for both of us. As I am working on the pancakes, bacon and scrambled eggs I hear ruffling through his room so I know he is up and should be here shortly, just knowing that my mind eases and my heart warms up.

I turn on the coffee machine with a flick of a finger while getting the bacon crunchy and putting everything on a plate as he comes down the stairs into the kitchen. He gives a big yawn as he finishes on closing his shirt and says "Hey big bro, ahead of me as usual I see?"

I chuckle at him and tell him "We can't all be sleepy heads little bro, some of us have to get everything for that big brain of yours to get energy for the day."

He seats down and starts chewing on a piece of bacon right away while grabbing his coffee mug before he finally says "Well I do have a big day today with quite a test to do."

I look at him while I drink my own coffee and says "Is that your way to 'beg me' into giving you my bacon now? I am sure you could come up with better than that." He grins at me and sticks his tongue out while I pull out the rest of the pan giving him the extra bacon I had prepared then tell him "I remembered about those tests lil bro so I had prepared more for you right away."

He chuckles as he chews on a pile of bacon and pancake and then tells me "Are we still going to the gym this evening big bro? I still want to be as big as you one day."

I chuckle at him with a nod, and as I am about to answer I hear my cellphone ringing in my bag. I grab it and see it's the swat emergency cell, I open it and say "Can't you guys do anything without me sincerely I am just an inspector..."

I get a high pitch chuckle in answer from the other side then a female voice says "Come on big sexy ice man, you know not everyone got an aim like yours." It's Serena Williams, an always laughing and smiling girl, which dispatches the team from the swat. She then adds "come on it's a hostage situation in a hotel, you are our best support chance."

I sigh and look at Vincent with his worried look on his face. He looks down and knows what I will say "Okay... stop trying to brownnose me and just tell me where it is... but your guys GOT to start doing stuff on their own, I can't keep holding their hands." Then I hang up once I got the address before I take a look at him, his smile his gone and I smell the worry going through his scent. So I get up and hold him close in my arms silently for a few minutes before I tell him "I will be at the gym this evening after your school lil bro I swear. We meet there okay?"

He gives me a little smile and says "I got faith in you big bro... be careful." I nod at him then grab my bag and my keys to head out toward the door.

I put my jacket on and go toward my motorcycle. As soon as I attached my bag on the side of it and put my helmet on I start it and speed as fast as I can toward the address Serena sent me. Knowing more or less the place it is I can understand why they need me on that one in a way. Not only it's a pretty "tight corner" with not a lot of place for a sniper to put himself but the worst for a sniper is the wind coming from the lake side of the city that messes up most aim. Yep "most aims" as I said, being trained from the desert I am used to aim through tempest pretty accurately even. Once I arrive, 30 minutes later, they give me the regular equipment of bulletproof jacket, headset and talkies. I look at the vicinities where I can place myself for the best angle and realize that the building in front is the obvious choice.

It might sound easy like that but there is no roof access from the inside and they aren't letting any helicopter get close to do that in a more regular way. So now I understand even more why they asked my help. I shake my mane and give a big sigh before I go toward the back of the building without further ceremony. Using the gutters, windows, and balcony and thanks to my training I am slowly climb up the seven floor building. Thinking people do that to get their adrenaline pumping and me I do that for necessity... sincerely I would pass if I had a choice in the matter. Took me around 20 minutes to climb on top safely and get an above view of the situation, I prepare my rifle and lay low on the rooftop to aim down at them, seeing each of my target I give them the green light and say "I count 6 on different windows, I can get them in 2 minutes top, maybe less if they are stupid."

To that Serena chuckles in my ear "Wouldn't expect any less than that from you big guy." And then she gets yelled at by the chief of the team below me for piercing his eardrums. I swear some bird anthros don't realize at times how much high pitch sounds they can pull out.

The more I look at the surrounding and situation the more I realize this really sound like a job I was the one of the very rare one able to pull. And for sure the only one in city that have a chance to do it by disarming and not killing. Thinking that suddenly gives me an uneasy feeling in the back of my mind, so I start looking through the windows once more to calm myself. I get back in the "Ice Bullet" state of mind, but can't help wondering if I am not the target at this point. I keep checking at any details I can see through the windows, and realize that they are a lot of items I am pretty sure I saw during my times in war, but then something else attracts my attention. I see some of the fur on the arms, with some designs that I am sure I know. They really don't remind me good stuff at all at that point but I don't manage to reconnect the dots of where or when it was.

I keep concentrating and deciding the order I need to take care of their weapons to help the team below me. Just hoping, at that point, that if we can get them alive I can get my answers at the same time. The chief of the team finally gives me the signal an hour later and I just grumble my answer before I start shooting their weapon to disable them and startle them. The last one of the six on the windows finally understand that something is happening and retreats behind a wall, so in automatic reaction I just do a rebound shot and from the scream I think I wounded him. Staying ready in case of any of them trying to pull something "bigger" to do their deed and not get caught without fighting of course. Then I hear the last hint of where I knew those symbols: their war cry.

It was one of the most fanatic groups I ever faced during my times there; they even had something against me after all the time since I was "supposedly" the one most responsible of their losses. Worries grow through my spine at that realization and keep my ears open to all they say. It took an hour more for the team to finally get them all inside the building then the last drop falls in, one of them keeps repeating "With the help of god on our side we will crush the ice and his relatives." They were actually here after me and this was really a way to find me. Not that they know it's only a matter of time before... before they find him.

While the team arrests the group I pull out my emergency exit rope, tie it on a safe spot and go down as fast as possible. I don't even stop to give them back their equipment's, I just attach my riffle on the side on my bike and jump on it as fast as I can to go toward his school. Serena and the chief keep screaming in my ears for explanation the only answer I give them before I am out of reach for the talkies is "I have to go keep him safe before they get to his school, this was made to find me."

Vincent:
He just left 30 minutes ago and here I am already pacing the living room worried for him. I saw the face he made when he had to leave and every time I see that face all I want is to grab him in my arms and kiss him, tell him I am by his side and that I love him. I remember what the people at the orphanage kept telling me about him, how he was antisocial and not caring about anyone but me. They even tried to tell me to be careful around him. But I couldn't agree with them, I was seeing in him what others weren't digging for, or even caring to try. I had heard about what they call "War trauma", but with me... around me he seemed fine and over it. The problem was every time he had to turn back to that "ice mode"... I hate that nickname they gave him. It's so unlike the real him I know.

I decide to seat back down at the table and finish my breakfast fast before catching the bus to school. I have to keep my grades up to keep making him proud of me.

I start to rinse the dishes then grab my bag and go toward the closet to grab a jacket for today. Opening it I see his old motorcycle jacket and slowly reach up to rub the texture gently. I pull it out of the closet and start smelling his scent coming from it slowly. I put my bag on the floor and try the jacket on, quite bigger than me for sure but I don't care. He doesn't use it anymore and his scent is still on it, so I decide to wear it today and feel his presence and support near me. It's not that cold outside, but wearing his jacket makes me feel so much warmer and better inside. I grab my bag again, my keys and after closing everything I come out of the apartment and head toward the bus. On my way I wave to the people of the neighborhood I know and get the feeling that I got someone following me.

For a minute I think I am just getting paranoiac or something like that. Then I really realize that two people, and a car down the street, really have an odd behavior. I wonder if I should call for help and at that moment a friend for school, an otter I pretty much consider a close friend, just honks at me from his car. He waves to me to come over and tells me "Hey big fuzzy, thought it was you down the street. Want a ride toward school before our test?"

I chuckle at him and say "Sure if you don't mind fur all around on your seats." He pats the seat next to him so I open the door and sit with my bags between my legs.

As I put my seatbelt on he tells me "Nice jacket, it doesn't look especially new so I am gonna guess it's his, right?" I nod at him and get a whiff of his scent while I think of those odd guys again. Seeing I am lost in my own thoughts he adds "I bet you didn't tell him anything yet didn't you."

I know it's not a question but I still sigh and answer "No I didn't I admit it. It's just... not easy to tell him I see the differences when he is 'work mode' or with me. He always been the one taking care of me and now... I am afraid that if I tell him what I feel I might lose him too..."

While still driving through the traffic he pats my knee gently and tells me "I think he is way too attached to you to ever consider going on without you sincerely." Then to lighten up the mood he adds "This jacket looks awesome on you by the way, I think you should keep it from now on." Then he gives me a big smile and adds "I bet he would even feel honored that you wear it, why else would he have kept it after he bought a new one."

The idea of it makes me blush on the tip of my ears but I admit that with him it's a possibility after all. He is not the kind to keep something just because it was his first one. The rest of the drive is more normal than the start as we head toward our destination and we just talk about the incoming test then he parks at the school and we join our group of friends that are on the usual bench with their nose deep into their books.

Of course the moment they see us they all wave at us for some last minute help in understanding some parts of the past lessons.

So we all seat together and I get more compliments on the "famous jacket" until it's time for us to go and start our test 45 minutes later so we head and seat in our designed spots.

The moment I arrive I decide to keep the jacket on and get a good whiff of his scent, thinking about him and hoping he is okay before I just start concentrating my brain on that test. Wanting him proud of me. An hour into the test I lift my head up to crack my back and see something from the corner of my eyes. It's just a quick moment I am pretty sure there was someone looking toward my direction that hided right away when I looked toward it. I consider it's just me being paranoiac again and put my head down to finish the test seriously. I finish it with an hour to spare and just decide to reread my answers when I hear a voice I know very well screaming at someone in the corridor and I am pretty sure I hear my name too.

The coincidence is too much at this point, I get up and reunite my stuff before I give my copy back. And there, behind the door, he was there screaming at a supervisor that it was too important to lose time and he had to take me to a safer location or at least be by my side to keep me safe. The moment he sees me he grabs me into his arms tight.

The first thing he says once he gets over the joy is "Damn I am so glad you are okay, I was so worried."

I try to look at him in the eyes but he doesn't let me go so I say "Bro... if you don't let me breathe I might not be okay for long." He puts me back on the floor and looks around us worried still so I ask "Please tell me what's wrong big bro."

He just says "We don't really have the time right now but I promise I will when we are in a safer place." He then turns toward the supervisor and tell him "I am sorry but he won't be able to come to school for a few days for security reasons, be it the school's or his. I can't explain a whole lot right now but the city's swat team will call to explain you probably in an hour when they realize what is happening." The way he looks at the supervisor with his jaw's clenched and his eyes cold as ice, he even makes the guy shiver in worries but he isn't reacting and just goes into "ice mode" again.

I hate when he turns into that "ice guy", he isn't the scary guy like that. He is caring and loving, he is a warm guy that wants to protect people... do his job... take care of me, not an iceberg as he is probably showing with the school supervisor right now. I just wrap my arms around him and tell him "Please big bro... don't act like that with him. You are about to make him pee himself."

He gasps and realizes that he isn't in a "war zone" anymore, or at least not yet since how serious he is I can imagine something really bad is happening. He just looks down and grabs the guy's hand before he tells him "I am very sorry... I didn't wanted to scare you... just please reinforce the school security and I will ask the swat and police squad to come help you guys. I am... very sorry." He then turns around and puts an arm around my shoulder before he tells me "Let's go get everything you need from your locker... we better not leave anything here that you might need or want to keep with you."

I look at him worried and tell him "It is that bad big bro?"

He just tightens his hand around my shoulder and says "It's not good news for sure... someone from my past." He then looks down and says "I am very sorry... you are in danger because of me right now."

At this point I just lean my head on him while we walk and tell him "It's not your fault big bro... you just did your job back then." I then grab his hand and twine my fingers between his before I add "You took care of me... and I don't regret any moments except the moments we aren't together." Then without a warning I turn his head around and start kissing him on the lips.

His eyes widen in surprise but he doesn't stop me. He just keeps holding me close to him but doesn't seem to want to push me away, for me the time stops. And even if my life is in danger, I am glad I had the courage to show him what I felt for him in a not possible way to misunderstand it.

Tyron:
I can't believe this is happening right now. I always had feelings for him, and wanted him near me. But I was so not expecting that to happen. Especially now.

This day was already so full of surprises, first those "ghosts from my past", and now this. The little guy I considered my little brother since so long is kissing me. And really not a "brotherly kiss" kind of way, does it means what I think it means? I don't know, I am not sure at all of anything at that moment. Except that this kiss feels good. It's like heaven and hell at the same time and I don't dare to push him away.

But then I remember all that is happening right now and I have to make it stop. I gently push him back and look at him in the eyes. I see he is worried and I just put my hand on his cheek with the nicest smile I can before I tell him "Lil bro... no Vincent... I got your message loud and clear. And I really want us to talk about it and share our feelings like you got no idea. But right now your life is still in danger and we still got to get out of here as fast as we can."

He gives me a small smile and looks down before he says "I... understand."

At this point I know he misunderstood what I meant, so I just lift his chin up gently and give him another soft kiss. It's shorter but enough to get my point across. Then I tell him "I don't think you got it fully, all I am saying is... that we need to get away from here fast." His smile is brighter as we head toward his locker and grab all his stuff before we go toward my motorcycle that I had, literally, parked inside the school building. While he is going through his locker I take off the bullet proof jacket so he can wear it instead of me and then pull out my cellphone. I do the Swat dispatch number to warn Serena. Of course the moment she answers she starts those high pitch sounds into my ear. I grunt and tell her "Can you hold off the squealing for the sake of my ears for a minute and let me explain you what is going on?"

After she calmed down and let me explain the situation to her she says "Okay we will warn the police stations to keep an eye out in the city and send a team to protect the school in case. But... for you both, are you in need of help?"

I look at Vincent while he puts on the bullet proof vest and tell her "I got all I need in our apartment; the windows and entrance are secured so we will be in there. We might just need some way to get food deliveries. I don't think he would enjoy the military rations I stocked up." To that I can't help but chuckles as I see him making a face and sticking his tongue out in disgust. She then gives a lower chuckle than usual and agrees that we will work something out. Once his bag is fully ready with all his stuff we make our way to my motorcycle to make an exit.

As we head toward my motorcycle parked in the lobby, he looks at me and says "I should probably mention something in case. I thought I was getting paranoid but now I am pretty sure that some people were following me this morning on the streets." After a few seconds he takes a deep breath and adds "I am also pretty sure I saw someone staring at me through the window during the test."

Earring that I just gasp and grab him by the arm a bit more roughly to make him run "Shit... this means they are most probably already onto us right now. We have to get away FAST..."

When we finally reach my bike I tell him "Hold me as tight as you can because this will be very bumpy." Then I make him seat in front of me so that I can protect him. Not waiting an answer from him I just start the bike and break through the front window of the lobby without warning. Just as I expected the moment we are out I hear gunshots toward our direction. Those jackasses don't even care for innocents I swear. I dodge the best I can and pass in the middle of parking lots hoping the cars stopped there will stop them. Or at least slow them a bit. Once we reach the top of the parking lot I tell him "You better close your eyes Vincent... there is only one way out from here now." I turn the bike around and face a sport car that is on the edge of the parking lot. My plan is basic, even if crazy as hell, use that car as a ramp to launch us toward the highway in front of us. I make the engine rumble and start speeding as fast as I can toward the sport car while he lowers his head against the windshield of my motorcycle. The moment we arrive on the said car my plan works and we are flying from the parking lot toward the highway intersection. As we land I spin around the direction for our apartment but the moment I see our exit I see they already are waiting for us there.

Seeing that I know that slowing down gets us as seating ducks just in their hands ready to get cooked. I start pushing the engine and go in quick changes of directions toward them. The moment I think I am finally getting through it a grenade makes us fly on the side. As we are in the air and my bike is sent against a wall I grab Vincent in my arms and roll us around behind a wall. I look at him as we land and realize he is okay just a bit stunned so I just put him safely behind me and call Serena with my cell. I don't even talk to her just put the phone in Vincent's jacket and let her hear the gunshots around us to let her know we need help. They should, normally, be able to track us with it.

While I can hear some of them starting to set themselves around us to box us and be able to finish us at their own decision, in other words they can't care less about our surroundings. They want me dead and that's at any cost. I reach over discretely to catch the bag holding my rifle and pull it toward me. While with one hand I unzip the bag I check I still have my knife and gun, feeling a relieve washing over me as I still feel their familiar shapes. I pull out the rifle and see that it's still in a good shape even if the visor is broken. At this point I just don't care I am just happy to have it with me. I pull Vincent inside a shop with me and put him behind some shelves before I decide it's time that I attack them unless I want them to really be cornering us.

I get up from where I left Vincent and decide to go in another corner of the shop after putting my rifle on my back safely. I have to get them away from him at any cost, and trying to snipe them would be useless in this location. So I guess all I can rely now is smartness and hand to hand combat... if I make it out of this place I got us. I look around and see ventilations that might allow me to get in the street to attack them from a side they won't expect.

I get up there and slowly and crawl my way back in the side street. As expecting they are all watching toward the shop and don't look where I am standing. I slowly get down the street and work my way a few cars back behind a van that is standing at an angle more or less behind them. I pull out my rifle and decide to do some instinct shots on them with the, very little, ammo I got left for it. I see most of them got some kind of gun that I can't really see the model from here. What bothers me most is that one of them got literally a rocket launcher and two others got shot guns.

I check again and see I got so far 5 bullets, I might be able to use 3 with the recharge time before they all attack me. They are ten in front of me, maybe a few more hiding and I know I want to get rid of that damn rocket launcher before anything else. If I can have the two shotguns too, by miracle or pure luck, that is icing on the cake to my point of view for sure. I give my best to aim, despite the broken lens, toward my first target. I know what I want at that moment is a "double shot": disable the launcher and if possible the one holding it.

As I am about to shoot at it I realize something at my advantage. To be faster in recharging his "toy" he left some extra rockets right next to his feet on the floor. Armed or not if I shoot at one of those two right next to him I am sure to make quite enough fireworks to kill at least 3 to 5 of those guys and wound up or at least disorient the others for a few minutes.

I breathe slowly and deeply as I aim and take mental notes of where my opponents are. Then I suddenly hold my breath and aim for one of the rocket while praying that my riffle won't fail me now. I manage to get the said rocket I wanted and make it explode taking with it 2 cars and 4 guys between the fire and the explosion. As I start running toward the others I make a mental note that my riffle is off by a few degrees on the right in case I still going to need it.

I never thought I would be so happy about having all those years of training behind me as I was now that I am fighting against those guys outnumbered. To tell the truth I would probably not have made it if the explosion hadn't scared them that badly or injured. I use my riffle as a staff to hit them if I am not kicking them and leaving them on the floor. I keep on fighting and calculating my next move as the usual "ice bullet mode" takes over me during the fight.

A few minutes later I might have a few cracked bones and bruises on my body but I am still in better shape than them.

The bigger problem is the more I look around the more I am sure one of them is missing. And there is the moment I hear something I really would never want to ever. The guy is coming out from the inside of the shop and holds Vincent by the throat with a gun on his head while poor Vincent is struggling and kicking all he can to get free from the guy.

He as a smirk on his face when he says "Now you are going to throw that 'soulless weapon' of yours on the floor and be very nice if you don't want that little guy to have an extra ventilation hole."

I know I have to save the most time I can to find a way to save him now. But damn it negotiation is not my forte at all. I slowly put my rifle on the floor and tell him "Why taking it out on him... you know it's me you want to add that 'extra ventilation' onto."

He starts with a chuckle and then goes into a full megalomaniac laugh before he says "True... so very true. But there is a little catch on that. I want to see you suffer... I want to see pain on your face for all the ones you killed in our group. God asked for it... their BLOOD ask for it." I still look intently at him and don't take my eyes of him; I am pretty much "ice in full mode" at that moment. He growls at me and says "You should know too that it's in my nature to torture my enemies."

As he says that he pulls out 3 daggers that he throws at me. One hit my shoulder; a second gets into my hip and the third gets into my stomach. I flinch in pain but still do my best to not get on my knees just yet, a few seconds later I tell him "I didn't knew you could use toothpicks that way."

His growl gets more deep as he says "You really never know when to quit don't you? You don't have your trusted sniper... your left arm is immobilized AND I got a hold of your 'lil brother' so..." As he finishes his speech he gives a lick along the cheek of Vincent and then adds "You... are DEAD you heretic."

I make a show to cringe in pain and hold my hip and stomach around his daggers before I tell him "Well big guy... I got to tell you about 'My nature' too since you told me yours." He looks at me with a playful smirk before he throws another knife in my right lung and, after coughing some blood on the floor, I add "Well for starter I been called 'ice bullet' all this year... I wonder if you know why." I look at him in the eye and add "It's mostly because I never hesitate to do anything to reach my goal."

I then reach slowly in my back and tell him, while still holding his eyes on me, I add "I don't use chopsticks unlike you... and I can use both arms to get my target." As I finish my sentence I grab my army knife attached on my back and throw it directly on his forehead, right next to Wuffy ear.

Seeing I managed to save him I just fall, face first, on the floor passing out.

Vincent:

I don't know what happened, we had a kind of accident and I woke up being dragged out by a big hyena that was holding me hostage in front of Tyron. Then when I saw Tyron ending up with some daggers in his body I closed my eyes and started crying. A minute after that the guy that was threatening me is dead, with Tyron's knife in his forehead and I just have time to see Tyron falling on the floor.

I don't understand what happened, all I know is that I am crying my heart out and screaming his name as I run toward him as fast as I can due to some bruises caused by the crash. As I am on my knees next to him trying to get him to open his eyes, seeing the blood all around him and the fire due to an explosion a very high pitch voice, coming out of nowhere, gets my attention. "Hey kiddo pick-up that phone and talk to me, are you both okay?"

For a minute I look around me and wonder what it could be, and then I realize I have Tyron's phone in my pocket that is transmitting with someone. I look at the screen and see written "Serena Swat" as an ongoing call. I pick it up and tell her "PLEASE... you have to get an ambulance here... he is bleeding very badly and got daggers in his body because of me... pl... please..."

I hear a gasp on the phone and some very speedy clicking on a kind of keyboard then she starts talking to me very softly again. "Okay, stay calm they already are on their way since I heard the first shot on the phone." She then adds "I just warned them about what you told me, so stay calm and don't move him too much and don't pull out the daggers. It might cause more blood loss."

Just after she finishes saying that I hear different sirens coming in the vicinities. As they arrive they force me away from him to take care of my bruises and start working on him. An hour later they finally let me go to wait while he is in surgery. I start passing back and forth in the waiting room alone and worried. Not even able to stop the tears when my friend Brian, the otter, arrives and grabs me in his arms telling me he heard what happened on the news. A few minutes later a very shiny blue lady bird with lots of jewelry arrives and introduces herself as Serena Williams. Took me a good 10 minutes to make her stop apologizing because she kept calling him for help for the swat missions.

4 hours later the doctor finally comes out and tell us that they did all they could, now it depended on him. Serena had pulled some strings to get him into an independent room with a protection service, plus she didn't let them any choice about me being able to stay with him.

There I was laying my head right next to him, praying to whoever might hear me, holding his hand and begging him to wake up and not leave me alone too. I am still crying, not letting his hand go and muttering my prayers when I hear a voice coming out softly right next to me "Like hell... I would leave you alone... I swore to take care of you... didn't I..."

My head shots up and I see him with his eyes slightly open and trying to smile at me gently. I had to use all my will to not jump in his arms at that moment so I wouldn't hurt him more or open the stitches. After drying my tears and catching my breath I finally tell him "My god... you really scared me to death you know. I thought I had lost you."

He slowly does his best to reach up my cheek with his hand and rub it softly "I was... afraid of... losing you too... you know." He then starts cringing and crying before he adds "Because of me... of what I did... of my past... you nearly died." He then turns his head away from me and adds "I nearly lost... the only person... I ever loved..."

I get up and pull back his chin gently toward me telling him "Please look at me." When he finally does I give him a big smile and say "You did all that 'past' because of me, I am the one to blame in a way for that not you. You wanted to take care of me this is why you did all that, and you didn't pick the missions they sent you. So please... stop thinking it's your fault." I then start crying and add "I won't ever bother you I promise, I will be good and won't force anything on you. I will keep making you proud at school, get a job even, anything you would ask me... but please." I take a deep breath and then say "Don't make me go away from you, I will even train to defend myself."

He looks surprised at me and some tears are coming out of his eyes too before he says "But... I come with a... pretty heavy package. It's... dangerous for you... to stay with me." I see him cringe in pain and he adds "More people of my past... might come out one day."

I shake my head and say "I don't care... I just want to stay by your side that's all I ever wanted."

He smiles at me and says "This is... all I ever... wanted too Vincent." He then moves a little bit on the side of his bed and tells me "Please... come in my arms so... I can have you close to me while I try to sleep... I want to know... this wasn't a dream..."

I gently get on the bed right next to him and let him hold me tight with his good arm while we both finally relax. Just before dozing off he whispers "I love you." into one of my ear. To which I answer "I love you most." with a big goofy smile on my face.

ABOUT THE AUTHORS

N. "Karmakat" Franzetti is a 34 year old French lion that been through different schools. Starting from accounting, then commercial he finally ended up in his passion the art and writing at a later age. He discovered the furry world at a young age but didn't know it for what it was until his 21st year. He now lives in the south of France with his Californian wife/editor and their 4 dogs. He does his best to live his passion and put his wild imagination on paper, be it in word or images, to be able to share it with the world.

"Behemel Fatereaver" is a 26 year old writer from the U.S. Having recently graduated from college, now is seeking to become a writer in the pro field. In his life, he had taken an interest in fur fandom as many fantasy novels show anthropomorphic characteristics, including mythology. He is a creative, an imaginative soul that is constantly striving to create new stories and concepts. Including, poetry, screen writing, fantasy fiction, science fiction, as well as plans for comic books. A good friend to Karmakat, and inspired by him and his friends with the characters they created, Karmakat being a big inspiration to the creation of Behemel as a character.

Xi "Wuffy" Silverwind is a twenty-three year old biologist-in-training from the United States. After many years of going it as a lone folf, he now joins the Silverwind family as a French lion's long lost little brother. Many years have passed since then but now he is ready to write it down as the whole chronicles of this family's crazy adventures. For it was them, his spangle, that kept him brave and steadfast when he was afraid.

ABOUT THE ARTIST

"Jake lioner" cute Finish lion, works for treats or scratches by the fire in long evenings of winter. Doesn't mind a beer at times and even a good laugh or singing along. Just watch out he is very shy and might need a hole to hide in case of compliments. Engaged with his wonderful Portlandian wolf.